The Complete Guide to

ENGLISH
SPELLING
RULES

By

John J. Fulford B.Ed. M.A.

Published by
ASTORIA PRESS

In each of the countries peopled by Englishmen,

a distinct dialect will gradually be formed; the principal of which

will be that of the United States. In fifty years from this time

American English will be spoken by more people, than any other

dialect of the language, and in one hundred and thirty years, by more

people than any other language on the globe....

NOAH WEBSTER, 1806

TABLE OF CONTENTS

Preface

Although English is described as a Germanic language, barely half of English words are of Germanic origin. English is a polyglot language that has borrowed words from almost every other language across the globe. The result is an extraordinary mixture of spellings that are either a great irritation or a source of fascination to the student. However, time and usage have tended to blend all the various spellings into a number of distinct groups, each of which have their own rules.

This book attempts to show that English spelling is not an illogical mish-mash of sounds and letters. On the contrary, English spelling does indeed have logical rules that govern how the words are spelled.

Many people believe that there can only be guides to English spelling and that because of its complexity, strict rules could not possibly exist. But I believe this to be illogical. English is the most important language in the world. It's used in both diplomacy and international business and in every form of communication. When every word in a written communication must be clear and unambiguous, it is obvious that spelling must follow basic rules.

For a spelling rule to have validity, it must prove to be correct in a very high percentage of cases. When the number of exceptions to the rule is too high, then the rule is not valid. Almost all the spelling rules in this book are valid to a very high level. At least two of the rules are completely valid and have no exceptions whatsoever.

Because of the unique history of the language there are often exceptions to many of the rules, but when compared to the number of words that do indeed follow the rule, these exceptions often prove to be quite rare. It is interesting to note that when a particular spelling changes or an incorrect spelling becomes popular, it is often a move toward the spelling rule than a move away. It is clear that those who use the language want conformity to logical spelling rules.

Strange as it may seem, considering the importance of spelling, not much school time is devoted to spelling. Almost all the formal instruction is in the primary grades, and this usually consists of the memorization of a weekly list of twenty words. The emphasis is on rote memorization and the students are given little if any explanation of why the words are spelled that way. The amount of time devoted to spelling decreases in the middle grades, and in high school it is not taught as a subject. There are no college or university courses in spelling, nor are students in teacher training colleges given spelling proficiency tests. The result is that many classroom teachers may be poorly equipped to teach spelling. Adults who are good spellers will find that their skill is due to constant reading rather than any actual study of spelling. They remember the correct way to spell a word and perhaps, by recognizing the root word and the various affixes, they can trace the origin of the word. But they do not know why the word is spelled that way.

While this book is intended as a valuable textbook for students of English, I hope that readers who already have a good grasp of the English language will find it extremely interesting and that it helps illuminate a long neglected corner of the English language.

Introduction

$\mathcal{E}$nglish has been described as a "borrowing" language, and this is undeniably true. Although English is called a Germanic language, probably only half the words in the dictionary are of Germanic origin. The rest we have acquired from Latin and a score of other languages. English is thus a polyglot language that has always borrowed words from other languages and always will, so that today we can say that almost every language in the world has contributed at least a few words to English.

The Germans and Scandinavians, who invaded Britain after the Romans departed, each brought a different dialect, sometimes even a different language. There were Angles and Saxons from what is now Germany, Jutes and Danes from the land we now call Denmark, Frisians from the Netherlands, and Vikings from Norway and Sweden. Although the invaders all strove to carve out separate kingdoms on the island they had invaded, their languages gradually blended into a common tongue, but one with many regional variations. This was the period that produced the richness and the extraordinary diversity of regional accents and dialects that exist to this day in the British Isles.

The French that the Normans brought to England was not quite the same as the French spoken in other parts of France. This is because the Normans were descendants of the "Northmen," or Vikings, who had settled in France. But their language was undeniably French, and it infused the Anglo-Saxon language with a very heavy dose of Latin-based words.

More Latin words arrived during the medieval period, when Latin was the international language of Europe, and the church, the universities, diplomacy, law, commerce, and many governments conducted their business in Latin. With the renewed interest in the classics during the Renaissance and the surge in literacy, Greek also became a subject of study and it too gave us many words.

The English language absorbed countless thousands of these new words, and while many of them were adapted to fit English speech patterns or grammar, quite a few remained untouched. As the English people became more involved in Continental affairs more new words filtered into their language, and if these words appeared to have value they were eagerly adopted. This pattern of adopt and adapt can be traced back to the earliest years and has served the language well.

War and trade also added large numbers of new words to the English language as ships manned by English-speaking sailors, both commercial and naval, ventured far and wide and set up trading stations or military outposts. With the growth of the British Empire, the pace accelerated and the English language spread around the globe. Each contact with another culture and another language almost always resulted in the acquisition of yet more new words. Meanwhile, in the New World, English-speaking North Americans were adding their own fascinating collection of new words with new meanings and new spellings.

For centuries, the English language has thus accumulated words rather like the mythical dragon adding constantly to its hoard, no matter the origin of the treasure. Not satisfied with just one word to describe an object or an action, the language eagerly snatched yet another and another. Today the English language has more words than any of the Romance or Germanic languages and probably more than any other major language.

There is no disputing the fact that English is the most important language in the world today. It is an international language that has a number of advantages over most other languages. English grammar is quite simple, almost all the nouns are neuter, the subjunctive hardly exists, the difference between formal and informal address is rarely used, contractions are used extensively, the possessive is usually contracted, and we simply add a word to create the future tense. English is a simple and uncomplicated language that is easily learned and, when used correctly, permits clear communication with little chance of serious misunderstanding.

For centuries, there was general illiteracy and spelling was not important. Even after the invention of the printing press, when the ability to read and write became more common, the meaning of a word and its pronunciation were of prime importance, but how the word was spelled was not important. Well into the 18th century, most writers spelled words the way they thought they should be spelled. This, unfortunately, is reflected all too often in modern spelling.

Dr. Samuel Johnson did not, as many people believe, write the first dictionary of the English language. There had been previous attempts but they were quite limited in scope and cannot be compared to the masterpiece that Johnson produced. Unfortunately, Dr. Johnson appeared on the stage of history at the wrong time.

The 18th century was a time of turmoil and transition during which the English language was changing rapidly. Up to that time, English had not been taken very seriously by the upper classes, who learned Latin and Greek in school and greatly admired one's ability to converse in French. However, the writers and thinkers of that period were beginning to take a careful look at the English language and especially at the sad state of English spelling. To correct obvious errors, some writers tried to apply the rules of Latin or French, whereas others looked back to Shakespeare and

The Germans and Scandinavians, who invaded Britain after the Romans departed, each brought a different dialect, sometimes even a different language.

some delved into the Anglo-Saxon or even German for the correct spelling of English words, producing such words as *musique* or *musick*. But their efforts were wasted. The version of English spoken in southeastern England was rapidly being accepted as the language of all England, and if it had been left alone to evolve and mature, we can speculate that English spelling would also have evolved.

However, the good Dr. Johnson, who was born in 1709, produced his masterpiece right in the middle of this period of change and, in effect, helped to freeze English spelling. There was a move at that time to standardize spelling, and one of the more famous proponents of standardization was Johnson's patron, Lord Chesterfield. Unfortunately, he and the doctor did not agree on many matters. Johnson heaped scorn on the very idea that spelling could be regulated. He wrote, "*may the lexicographer be derided who ... shall imagine that his dictionary can embalm his language and secure it from corruption and decay....*"

Johnson contented himself with explaining the meanings of the words in his dictionary with numerous quotations and brilliant observations. He showed how the words were to be used, but as to the spelling, he preferred the status quo. Not only did he retain obvious inconsistencies, but he even added to them. His most famous was his addition of the letter *p* to *receipt*. Despite his foibles, Dr. Johnson must be recognized as one of the great men of English literature.

NOAH WEBSTER

Noah Webster was born in 1758 in Connecticut almost fifty years after Dr. Johnson. A product of impeccable Puritan and Pilgrim English ancestry, he was nevertheless a staunchly patriotic Yankee and an enthusiastic supporter of the American Revolution. He was a brilliant student and a prolific writer and publisher who made many influential friends, including George Washington. Webster traveled widely throughout the young republic and, among other things, persuaded Congress to pass the first copyright laws. He was a schoolmaster with an intense interest in language reform.

In 1786, Webster was in Philadelphia listening to Benjamin Franklin's proposal for a completely new alphabet. Franklin had even had special type made up but, fortunately, Webster rejected the idea as too radical. Webster had already produced a grammar book, and in 1783 he produced his first spelling

Today the English language has more words than any of the Romance or Germanic languages and probably more than any other major language.

book, which soon became extremely popular as the *American Spelling Book* or Webster's *Blue-Backed Speller.*

Webster made frequent revisions to his spelling book, changing, improving, and enlarging, but always striving to *"extirpate the improprieties ... to reform the abuses and corruptions which ... tincture the conversation."*[1] His spelling book quickly became one of the best selling books in the history of American publishing. At one time there were over a hundred publishers producing the book legally and countless pirated editions. It was in continuous publication for well over one hundred years.

The difference between Dr. Johnson and Noah Webster is clear. The former was primarily interested in the meaning of the words and their correct usage. To Dr. Johnson, the spelling was of little importance. The practical American, on the other hand, while stressing correct usage, was very interested in correct pronunciation and spelling. Webster, who had traveled in Europe, was fluent in a number of languages and had studied Anglo-Saxon, so his suggestions as to the "cleansing" of the English language were based on serious study. Although many of his original improvements in spelling were never adopted, it is surprising just how many of them were eventually accepted. Many of the words in our current dictionaries, on both sides of the Atlantic, are spelled according to Webster. In the introduction to his dictionary in 1806 Noah Webster wrote with uncanny foresight:

> *In each of the countries peopled by Englishmen, a distinct dialect will gradually be formed; the principal of which will be that of the United States. In fifty years from this time American English will be spoken by more people, than any other dialect of the language, and in one hundred and thirty years, by more people than any other language on the globe....*[2]

SPELLING REFORM

Noah Webster was the first lexicographer to attempt to bring some kind of order to English spelling. His arguments were based on a thorough knowledge of the subject and laced with a heavy dose of common sense. In the preface to

> The version of English spoken in southeastern England was rapidly being accepted as the language of all England, and if it had been left alone to evolve and mature, we can speculate that English spelling would also have evolved.

---

1 All quotations are taken from Noah Webster's twenty page preface to his *Compendious Dictionary of the English Language*, New York: Crown Publishers, 1970 (originally published in New Haven, Connecticut, in January, 1806).

2 Webster, 1806, p. xxii.

his *Compendious Dictionary of the English Language,* he took great pains to explain his reasoning. Let us use his words to look first at the *centre-center, theatre-theater* problem.

> *We have a few words of another class which remain as outlaws in orthography. These are such as end in* re, *as* sceptre, theatre, metre, mitre, nitre, lustre, sepulchre, spectre, *and a few others.... It is among the inconsistencies which meet our observation in every part of orthography that the French* nombre, chambre, disastre, disordre, etc. ... *should be converted into* number, chamber, disaster, disorder, etc. *confirmable to the pronunciation, and that* lustre, sceptre, metre, *and a few others should be permitted to wear their foreign livery*[3].

He supports this statement by pointing out that the great English writers Newton, Dryden, Shaftsbury, Hook, Middleton, et al., wrote these words in the "regular English manner."

Further on, Webster writes:
> *The present practice is not only contrary to the general uniformity... but is inconsistent with itself; for Peter, a proper name, is always written in the English manner; while* salt petre, *the word, derived from the same original, is written in the French manner.* Metre *also retains its French spelling, while the same word in composition, as in diameter, barometer, and thermometer, is conformed to the English orthography. Such palpable inconsistencies and preposterous anomalies do no honor to English literature, but very much perplex the student, and offend the man of taste.*[4]

From this, we can see that Webster, far from demanding radical change, was only insisting that English spelling conform to historical spelling rules. He was actually very conservative.

We may again use Noah Webster's own words in the problem of *labor-labour* and *honor-honour* :

The difference between Dr. Johnson and Noah Webster is clear. The former was primarily interested in the meaning of the words and their correct usage. To Dr. Johnson, the spelling was of little importance. The practical American, on the other hand, while stressing correct usage, was very interested in correct pronunciation and spelling.

---

3 Webster, 1806, p. vii.
4 Webster, 1806, pp. viii-ix.

> *To purify our orthography from corruptions and restore to words their genuine spelling, we ought to reject u from honor, candor, error, and others of this class. Under the Norman princes... to preserve a trace of their originals, the o of the Latin honor, as well as the u of the French honeur was retained... our language was disfigured with a class of mongrels. splendour, inferiour, superiour, authour, and the like, which are neither Latin nor French, nor calculated to exhibit the English pronunciation.[5]*

He continues:

> *The palpable absurdity of inserting u in primitive words, when it must be omitted in the derivations, superiority, inferiority, and the like; for no person ever wrote superiourity, inferiourity...[6]*

Again we can see that Webster was demanding conformity in spelling including a strict adherence to the basic rules, for, as he wrote in an earlier paragraph, "Uniformity is a prime excellence in the rules of language."

Another interesting difference between English and American spelling is the double *l*. The spelling rule for doubling the consonant when adding a suffix is quite clear. Part of the rule states that in words of more than one syllable, the final consonant shall not be doubled unless the accent falls on the final syllable. For example, *regret–regretted*. British spelling adheres to this rule except when the word ends in an *l*. Then, for some yet to be explained reason, the rule is abandoned and the *l* is doubled no matter where the accent happens to be. For example, *travel–travelled*. This double *l* can be seen in other strange places, such as, *chili–chilli, woolen–woollen*.

However, there are at least half a dozen cases where the situation is reversed and the British spell the word with only one l, while the Americans, for no logical reason, spell it with two. For example:

BRITISH	AMERICAN	BRITISH	AMERICAN
instil	*instill*	*skilful*	*skillful*
wilful	*willful*	*distil*	*distill*
enrol	*enroll*	*fulfil*	*fulfill*
instal	*install*		

---

5 Webster, 1806, p. ix.
6 Webster, 1806, p. ix.

Noah Webster would have had something quite scathing to say about "such palpable inconsistencies and preposterous anomalies."

In American spelling, there is a conscious attempt to simplify while retaining the correct sound and meaning, especially in the case of multiple letters. British English still retains numerous examples of double consonants where a single consonant would be quite sufficient, for example, *worshipping* and *focuss*. American simplification extends especially to triple vowels. Whether they are diphthongs or not, we feel that two vowels should be enough to produce the desired sound. Fortunately, many of the British triple vowel words are slowly disappearing, for example, *diarrhoea–diarrhea* and *manoeuvre–maneuver*. Retaining an unneeded and unhelpful extra letter is illogical when we remember that the prime function of language is clear communication.

Since Noah Webster's time there have been a number of attempts to reform, or at least to improve, English spelling. They vary from the thoughtful to the ludicrous. At the present time there is a widespread belief that perhaps English spelling could be made more phonetic, despite the fact that English is not a completely phonetic language. Roughly half of our words are already spelled phonetically, but the other half could never be spelled according to the rules of phonics without utter chaos. In the words of the great writer Jonathan Swift,

> *Another cause ... which hath contributed not a little to the maiming of our language, is a foolish Opinion, advanced of late years, that we ought to spell exactly as we speak, which besides the obvious inconvenience of utterly destroying our Etymology, would be a thing we should never see the end of.*[7]

This is not to say that spelling is sacrosanct and should never be allowed to change; on the contrary, our spelling is constantly changing, sometimes at glacial speed, other times quite rapidly. But not all change is for the better. A change in spelling is acceptable if it purges the original word of superfluous letters or illogical construction. Simplification is to be encouraged only if it does not change the meaning of the original word in any way. It is imperative that the new

---

7 Webster, 1806, p. 15.

spelling conform to the spelling rules and that it resemble the original word as closely as possible. Care should be taken to try to avoid the creation of yet another homophone or homograph.

Many attempts to reform English spelling have been targeted at the alphabet. George Bernard Shaw left the bulk of his fortune to a committee charged with producing a better alphabet, but with no success. On the other hand, the 19th century geniuses who produced the International Phonetic Alphabet were very successful and the IPA, has proved immensely valuable.

Probably the most famous person to tackle the problem was Benjamin Franklin. Although he was a friend of Noah Webster and an enthusiastic supporter of Webster's work, he was much more radical than Webster. Franklin designed an alphabet containing six new letters, and he eliminated the *c* in favor of the *s* and the *k*. He showed his specially carved type to Webster, but Webster declined to use it. Initially, Webster had proposed quite a few revolutionary changes to English spelling, but the resistance that he encountered soon persuaded him that the average person was—and still is— not prepared to accept extraordinary changes to his or her mother tongue. Although Webster gradually modified his suggestions, quite a large number of his improvements were eventually accepted on both sides of the Atlantic.

MELVILLE (MELVIL) DEWEY

The second half of the 19th century saw a renewal of interest in spelling reform. In 1875, the American Philological Society, working with the Philological Society of London, formed a committee, and within a year, in August, 1876, the International Convention for the Amendment of English Orthography met in Philadelphia. There was great enthusiasm for the project. Leading scholars from the best American and British universities, as well as writers and statesmen from both sides of the Atlantic, hastened to support this worthwhile endeavor. Almost immediately, the Spelling Reform Association was formed and they quickly elected as its secretary the controversial genius Melville Dewey.

Dewey was an extremely interesting character whom we may perhaps call the first efficiency expert. While still an undergraduate at Amherst College he worked out a more efficient method for cataloging books. This eventually became the Dewey Decimal System, for which he is best remembered. He also helped found the American Library Association, was editor of numerous library journals, and in 1887 created the Columbia University School of Library Economy. He was twice elected president of the American Library Association.

Dewey did not limit himself to books and libraries. He was also an enthusiastic proponent of the metric system and worked long and hard to get the authorities to abandon the archaic English system of weights and measures and adopt the new, highly efficient metric system. His arguments were irrefutable, yet today, one hundred years later, the United States is the only industrialized country in the world to still cling to that ancient and cumbersome system.

Dewey took keen interest in anything that could be made more efficient. He was an advocate for the greater use of abbreviations, arguing logically that we use M.D. and Ph.D. without pronouncing the entire title and we always refer to the national capitol as Washington, D.C. Why not apply this simplification to other things? Today the U.S. Postal Service uses a two-letter abbreviation for every state in the union.

When the Spelling Reform Association was created, Dewey was in his element and, with his unbounded enthusiasm, he became the driving force behind the movement. He even changed his name to "Melvil," and, for a short period, wrote his name "*Dui*," though he eventually changed it back. When critics complained about the proposed changes he pointed out that *gossip, gizzard,* and *gospel* had once been spelled *ghossip, ghizzard,* and *ghospel,* so why not simplify *ghost* and *ghastly?* He reminded critics that English spelling constantly changes, almost always in the direction of simpler and more logical spelling. He once estimated that learning spelling wasted two to three years of the average student's schooling.

One editor poked fun at Dewey's suggestion that we drop the unnecessary *ue* in *catalogue* and asked what we should do when we drop the *ue* in *glue.* Apart from the fact that the editor was deliberately confusing the spelling rules, we see today that Dewey was correct. Catalog is now the accepted spelling.

The Greek *ph* that sometimes seems to saturate our spelling was another irritant to Dewey. If we have *fancy,* he asked, why do we still have *phantom?* Throughout his career he used *fonic* for *phonic* and urged the complete eradication of the *ph.*

Dewey saw at once that the spelling reform movement would need money to promulgate its views, and so he contacted Andrew Carnegie for financial support. Although Carnegie was putting large sums of his immense fortune into public libraries, he was still a hard-headed businessman. His letters to Dewey usually included demands to "show me some results." Dewy was persuasive, however, and Carnegie supported the reform movement, not only with hard cash but also with a steady stream of letters to the leading newspapers in support of spelling reform. By 1906, Carnegie had increased his support to a generous $15,000 per year.

In his demands for "results," Carnegie insisted that Dewey send him a list of influential persons who had positively affirmed that they had accepted and would use a minimum of ten of the new spellings. Interestingly, among the selected words were *catalog, decalog, demagog, pedagog, prolog,* and *program,* all of which are now fully accepted.

The spelling reform movement received enthusiastic support from numerous prestigious organizations. The American Association for the Advancement of Science, the National Education Association, and the Modern Language Association all supported reform and the powerful *Chicago Tribune* likewise threw its weight behind the campaign.

The movement soon caught the attention of Theodore Roosevelt, who was a friend of Andrew Carnegie. With his usual energy, Roosevelt leapt right in. He used many of the "reformed" words in his election campaign and, it is claimed, was the first to use *thru* instead of *through.* Cannily waiting until congress was safely out of session, the president gave a list of three hundred words to the government printers and ordered them to use only those spellings. There was an immediate uproar and, as soon as congress reconvened, the printers were ordered to go back to the original spellings.

As early as 1886, the reformers had begun to compile a list of amended spellings. Starting cautiously with only one dozen "crucial" words that included *tho, altho, thoro, thorofare, thru,* and *thruout,* they quickly compiled even longer lists so that within a very short while the list of amended spellings was about 3,600 words long. In 1898, the National Education Association gave its approval to the twelve crucial words. The Modern Language Association had done so five years earlier.

After the initial burst of enthusiasm, there followed years of hard work. Lists were compiled, committees were formed, experts argued endlessly, and a steady stream of letters and bulletins were sent out. The reformers worked hard to persuade publishers and editors of dictionaries to adopt the reformed spellings and *The Century Dictionary* was persuaded to add the new words as an appendix with an introduction, while the *Standard Dictionary of the English Language* (1893) incorporated all the amended spellings into its listings.

In 1915, there appeared *A Dictionary of Simplified Spelling from the New Standard Dictionary of the English Language; and Based on the United States Bureau of Education and the Rules of the American Philological Association and the Simplified Spelling Board.* It was hoped that this, along with other smaller dictionaries and word lists that had been previously published, would forever reform English spelling.

However, Andrew Carnegie died and with his death, the essential funding dried up. Oral support alone could not pay the bills and the Spelling Reform Association, under its able secretary Melvil Dewey, could not find another generous sponsor. The lack of support can, perhaps, be traced to the fact that Dewey was openly anti-Semitic and had made many enemies in the business community.

Some smaller groups tried valiantly to carry on the struggle, but more important international matters filled the newspapers. A new generation of professors appeared in the universities, and the publishers and editors began to look upon spelling reform as a lost cause. In England the Simplified Spelling Society, which was founded in 1908, still keeps the flag flying bravely, but it is essentially ignored, while in the United States, largest of the English speaking countries, spelling reform is rarely if ever discussed.

Unfortunately, the failure of the reform movement brought about a reaction. Beginning in the late 1930s, various self-proclaimed experts in the field of education declared spelling to be unimportant. By the 1960s, most school report cards no longer gave a grade for spelling. Teachers were told not to "waste time" teaching correct spelling, and the spelling bee and other spelling competitions were dropped from most school programs. Their place was taken by "sight reading" and "creative spelling" along with a serious but misguided reliance on phonics, with the tragic result that a whole generation of adults, including teachers, has grown up to believe the myth that English spelling has no rules and that trying to understand English spelling is therefore a waste of time.

Was spelling reform a wasted effort? The question begs to be asked. Most of the great names in academia on both sides of the Atlantic, supported by numerous respected societies and organizations, put long years of hard work into something that they truly believed was worthwhile. The movement received the support of statesmen and businessmen and quite a few editors, and yet today it appears to have been for nothing.

A number of good things did come from the renewed interest in spelling, the most important of which was the International Phonetic Alphabet, which consists of a separate symbol for every speech sound the human mouth is capable of producing, no matter what the position of the lips or the tongue. Obviously, there are a great number of these symbols and the IPA is astonishingly complex, but it works well and scholars across the globe, especially linguists, would be lost without it. A simplified version may be found in any good dictionary. Originating about 1860, the IPA has been improved and enlarged and is constantly being revised. Those thinkers of the past who longed for a completely new alphabet based purely on phonics now had what they wanted.

During the early years of the 20th century, there were many who seriously suggested that traditional alphabets should be abandoned and that the IPA, or a modified version of it, should be the basis of all written communication. The heady idea of an international alphabet caught on and, up to about the 1930s, dozens of small books were printed in the new alphabet, mostly in England and Germany. Unfortunately, the movement ran head-on against Esperanto, a language invented by the Polish philologist L. Zamenhof in 1887. Designed as an international language that did not require a special alphabet, it was enormously popular for a number of years. Esperanto is still enjoyed by many, even today, but it is doubtful that it will ever become a truly international language.

The spelling reformers had not wasted their time. It is true that the majority of the suggested new spellings were rejected or even laughed at, but it is also true that quite a few of the suggested spellings are today in general use or given as alternate spellings in most dictionaries. What is just as valuable in the long run is the realization that spelling can change and that new spellings could possibly be more logical and quite acceptable.

A good example is the advertising industry. Before the reform movement, most written advertising was pedantic, long winded, and verbose. The reform movement opened the floodgates, and new spellings, new words and new meanings poured from the printing presses. Much to the dismay of the purists, the advertising world took reform and phonics to its heart and proceeded to spell things in new and eye-catching ways. It still does.

One of the reasons that the spelling reform movement was not a complete success was British stubbornness. Many distinguished scholars from London and Oxford joined the movement at the very beginning and supported it to the very end, but it must be remembered that the British people had not yet accepted the completely logical spelling corrections that Noah Webster had introduced a century earlier. While the Americans were already using *color* and *center*, the British still had to be persuaded of the correctness of these and many other similar words. The delegates had to persuade their countrymen on the other side of the Atlantic, and in this they largely failed. At that time, when the British Empire was at the height of its power, the British saw the project as an American idea and almost completely ignored it. To this day, British dictionaries still largely ignore the improvements of Noah Webster and those that came from the spelling reform movement, although some dictionaries do mention them as Americanisms.

But Britain is changing rapidly. The isolation is gone. The younger generation see themselves as part of Europe and the world, and many Englishmen speak a second language and regularly go abroad for their holidays. The new generation does not reject the idea that perhaps the modern spellings make more sense than the traditional ones.

A careful study of the more than 3,000 words contained in the *Amended Spellings Recommended by the Philological Society of London and the American Philological Association* (1886) can be a surprisingly rewarding experience. The reformers did not fail, nor was their time wasted. They saw what was wrong with English spelling and they logically and systematically corrected the errors. The fact that the English-speaking world did not immediately accept all their recommendations does not mean that they did not do their work well. On the contrary, they did so thorough a job that the results were too many to be assimilated all at once.

The modern reader has to admire the logic of their thinking, but, at the same time, the reader is repulsed by the strangeness and, at times, the awkwardness of many of the proposed spellings. Changing one's language after spending nearly twenty years learning it is not an easy thing to do.

When criticized because many reformed words did not look like the original word, Melvil Dewey coined the phrase "visual prejudice." He was quite right. Good readers are visual readers, and the faster we read, the more we rely on word recognition. We are long past the stage where we sound out each syllable of every word and we barely glance at the outline of a word before instantly recognizing it. Aided by context, we recognize, understand, and process dozens of words in seconds. For this very reason, a typographical error or a spelling error usually stands out clearly and because it clashes with what we know to be correct, it interrupts our reading and is an irritant.

For example, let us take the words *scribbled* and *measurable*, which in the amended spelling appear as *scribld* and *mezurabl*. It is clear that this is the way they are pronounced and the loss of a few superfluous letters should make little difference. But they seem strange and clumsy. We are prejudiced in favor of the older, more illogical spelling. Noah Webster was correct when he wrote, "No great changes should be made at once ... but gradual change."

In their enthusiasm, the reformers attempted to eliminate all the illogicalities once and for all, as in the following examples.

Many words end in a silent *e* that performs no useful function. It does not modify the vowel that precedes it, nor is it sounded.

candle	candl	massive	massiv
bundle	bundl	proscriptive	proscriptiv
engine	engin	punitive	punitiv
practice	practis	subversive	subversiv

Unfortunately, this correction clashes with several spelling rules. Few, if any, commonly used English words end in a plain *v*, and when the *l* follows a consonant, it too is rarely alone. Usually it is *le*, *el*, or *al*.

Occasionally the *ed* of the past tense sounds like a *t*. The reformers spelled a great number of these words with a simple *t* and dropped the *e* from most of the others.

asked	askt	lived	livd
laughed	laft	faltered	falterd
jerked	jerkt	joggled	jogld
fished	fisht	killed	kild

Here again the improvements clash with the spelling rules. The past tense of English verbs is usually *ed*. The exceptions are actually very few. The *t* sound only occurs after certain letters and is quite rare. When the reader sees that final *ed*, it is instantly recognized as the past tense and complete understanding of the concept is instantaneous. In its place, the reformers gave us a confusing mixture of past tenses.

Double consonants are a major problem in English. Because few other languages are so cluttered with double consonants as English, the reformers removed as many as possible.

add	*ad*	*meddle*	*medl*
bull	*bul*	*puzzle*	*puzl*
cell	*cel*	*swelled*	*sweld*
kill	*kil*	*quibble*	*quibl*

Again, the spelling rule is quite clear as to when, and when not, to double the consonant, and the reformers ignored the fact that a double consonant usually indicates a short vowel. It appears that the reformers were torn between following the spelling rules while purging superfluous consonants on the one hand and simply abandoning all the spelling rules on the other. As a result, there are quite a few anomalies scattered throughout their list of amended spellings.

A major source of irritation in English spelling is the *ough, augh, igh* anachronism. This ancient spelling should have faded away centuries ago. The reformers purged it completely.

cough	*cof*	*haughty*	*hauty*
laugh	*laf*	*hiccough*	*hiccup*
through	*thru*	*plough*	*plow*
though	*tho*	*rough*	*ruf*

Here, we can only praise the reformers and wish they had modernized every single word in this group.

That Greek nuisance, the *ph*, was also eliminated. The reformers reasoned that because the Greeks used only one letter for that particular sound, we should do the same.

phonetic	*fonetic*	*phenomenon*	*fenomenon*
alphabet	*alfabet*	*phonograph*	*fonograf*
lymph	*lymf*	*pharmacy*	*farmacy*
digraph	*digraf*	*philosophy*	*filosofy*

For this, we can again praise the reformers.

There are times when g must be followed by a *u* in order to achieve the correct hard sound, but there are also numerous cases where the *u* is superfluous and the reformers removed it.

colleague	*colleag*	*analogue*	*analog*
guaranty	*garanty*	*catalogue*	*catalog*
guard	*gard*	*dialogue*	*dialog*
guild	*gild*	*synagogue*	*synagog*

Today, at least four of the examples given above are often spelled in the reformed manner.

French spellings, particularly suffixes, can be a hazard in English spelling and these also were eliminated wherever possible.

gazelle	*gazel*	*epaulette*	*epaulet*
gazette	*gazet*	*petit*	*petty*
cigarette	*cigaret*		

There were not many of these because Webster had eliminated most of them a century earlier.

Needless to say, there were numerous other changes made, including the removal of silent letters. They removed the silent *t* in *etch* and *crutch*. They did the same with the silent *b* in *debt* and *doubt*. The useless *h* in *ghost* and *ghastly* was exorcized, and even the *s* in *island* went its lonely way. There were, of course, vowel changes too numerous to list.

Some of the changes were quite strange. The word *school* was changed to *scool*, retaining the *c* where a *k* would have been more logical, yet the word *sceptic* was correctly respelled *skeptic*. Today this is the preferred spelling. Another logical spelling that was accepted almost immediately was *saltpeter* instead of *saltpetre*. Strangely enough, the committee made no change to *sceptre* except to transpose the *e* and the *r*, though they left the silent *c* in place. However, the word *scimitar* was changed to *cimitar* instead of the more logical *simitar*.

If we look at the work of the reformers from a purely logical point of view, we must agree that they did an excellent job. However, a language is more than just symbols on paper. It is much more personal. It is too deep a part of the culture of those who use it and who have spent a great deal of time and effort perfecting their use of it. Any tampering with something so important is bound to meet stiff resistance.

FOUR GUIDELINES FOR SPELLING REFORM

There are four basic points that should always be borne in mind when considering spelling changes. Perhaps if we look at the work of the reformers from this point of view, we may be able to see more clearly why their efforts were largely ignored.

(1) **"A change in spelling is acceptable if it purges the original word of superfluous letters or illogical construction."** It is clear that the reformers did this, often with excessive enthusiasm.

(2) **"Simplification is to be encouraged only if it does not change the meaning in any way or create yet another homophone or homograph."** Here the reformers made too many mistakes. Considering the high quality of the academics who made up most of the committees, it is truly astonishing the number of times that the reformed word was simply a homonym and bound to cause confusion.

heart	*hart*	*quay*	*key*	*plumb*	*plum*
bread	*bred*	*rhyme*	*rime*	*queue*	*cue*
bussed	*bust*	*chilled*	*child*	*scent*	*sent*
caste	*cast*	*joust*	*just*		

(3) **"In all cases it is imperative that the new spelling conform to the spelling rules."** It is all too clear that the spelling rules were largely ignored by the reformers. Perhaps they saw these rules as traditions that had to be broken in order to get the job done, or perhaps they hoped to create new spelling rules that were more logical. Whatever their reasoning, it is clear that they wasted little effort attempting to make their spellings conform to the traditional English spelling rules.

(4) **"...and that it resemble, as closely as possible, the original word."** In this vital matter, the reformers failed completely. There was little if any attempt to cater to the "visual prejudice" of the general public. Too many of the new words appear ungainly, awkward, and down right ugly. Many are so different in appearance that the reader has to pause a while in order to assimilate them. When all things are considered, it is probably this last factor that was mainly responsible for the lack of interest shown by the general public and the ultimate decline of the reform movement.

FOUR GUIDELINES FOR SPELLING REFORM

(1) A change in spelling is acceptable if it purges the original word of superfluous letters or illogical construction.

(2) Simplification is to be encouraged only if it does not change the meaning in any way or create yet another homophone or homograph.

(3) In all cases it is imperative that the new spelling conform to the spelling rules.

(4) "...and that it resemble, as closely as possible, the original word.

There is little doubt that elitism and snobbery were important factors in the defeat of the spelling reformers. At the time the reformers were working, the great cities of the eastern United States were swarming with new immigrants, most of whom were low-class laborers with just a smattering of English. In England and in America, the people who migrated to the cities from rural areas were hardly much better, as few had much education.

It can take up to twenty years for a person to acquire a near perfect grasp of English, and it usually takes both time and money, two things not available to the average working man at that time. The result was a small but powerful elite that read books, newspapers, and journals and prided itself on the ability to use both the spoken and the written word with ease and skill. The standard of literacy and fluency was very high indeed—for the few. This is not to say that it was only the children of the rich and powerful who were well educated. History is full of examples of men and women of very humble origins who acquired a near perfect grasp of the English language through extraordinary perseverance. Abraham Lincoln is an excellent example.

But the common working man, who was most in need of a better education, was not asked for his opinion of the work of the spelling reformers. The most violent criticism of reform came from newspaper editors, writers, and statesmen, all of whom saw it as an attack on that which they valued the most—their excellent grasp of English and their hard earned knowledge of its intricacies and subtleties. We could compare this resistance to the medieval guild masters protecting their craft and craftsmen from interlopers.

Today, when literacy is all but universal, we can look back with some astonishment at the way in which spelling reform was rejected and the virulence of those who opposed it. But has one short century made much difference? There is still a great deal of elitism involved in the use of English. One small grammatical error can lower a speaker in the eye of his listener; a little mispronunciation or the wrong accent can do the same. Poor sentence structure can ruin even the best article or e-mail, whereas the clever use of words can make the poorest argument sound convincing.

As for spelling, there is an almost primitive defensive reaction to any spelling mistake discovered in our morning newspaper. We are angry and indignant when we see spelling mistakes in any printed document, whether it is an official publication or merely a hand-delivered leaflet. This reaction occurs just as readily when the misspelled word is one of those ludicrous, illogical, un-phonetic words that should have been "reformed" centuries ago.

There are numerous publications that refuse to use any "modern" spelling. The editors seem to think that *analogue* is superior to *analog*, that *archaeology* with three vowels in a row is more correct than *archeology* with only two, and they shudder at *thru* and *lite*. Unfortunately, such reactionary thinking is not uncommon, even though it is historically and etymologically false and any attempt to radically "improve" English spelling will surely be met by stiff resistance based largely on visual prejudice. In the preface to his 1806 edition, Noah Webster wrote,

> *The opposers of reform, on the other hand, contend that no alterations should be made in orthography, as they would ... occasion inconvenience.... It is fortunate for the language and for those who use it, that this doctrine did not prevail in the reign of Henry the Fourth ... had all changes in spelling ceased at that period, what a spectacle of deformity would our language now exhibit! Every man ... knows that a living language must necessarily suffer gradual changes in its current words, and in pronunciation ... strange as it may seem the fact is undeniable, that the present doctrine that no change must be made in writing words, is destroying the benefits of an alphabet, The correct principal respecting changes in orthography seems to lie between these extremes of opinion. No great changes shall be made at once... But gradual changes to accommodate the written to the spoken language ... and especially when they purify words from corruptions...are not only proper but indispensable.[8]*

A Note on Usage in This Book

Throughout this book, I use the phrase "commonly used words." This needs a little explanation. The English language contains over half a million words, more than any other European language, and new words appear almost daily as old words change or disappear. No one person could

---

8   Webster, 1806, p. 4.

be familiar with the entire vocabulary. While the average educated person uses only a tiny fraction of these words, he or she is familiar with, and will recognize, a much greater number. Although the words used in this book can be found in any good dictionary, I have attempted to keep to a bare minimum the use of names, technical and scientific terms, and rare or obscure words.

I use the terms "stem" and "root" when referring to the basic word before affixes have been added. In the majority of cases, the stems will be recognizable words, but, over time, many of these words have vanished or been drastically changed, and yet the stem with its affix has remained. For example, we use the words invoke, provoke, and revoke, and it is clear that the in, pro, and re are prefixes. But the root word voke no longer exists.

CHAPTER I
Syllables

*C*lear and careful pronunciation is of immense value when one is faced with a spelling problem. Breaking a word into its component syllables is the best approach to clear pronunciation, which brings us to the question, just what is the correct way to divide a word into syllables?

Most dictionaries, texts, and guides are quite useless, as there are both complete confusion and numerous contradictions. If we look up a word in three different guides, we will probably get three different choices, sometimes four. This is unfortunate because correct syllabification is a great help to both correct pronunciation and correct spelling.

Words are merely sounds strung together to form recognizable combinations. The heart of each sound is a vowel or diphthong. The vowel sound will be either short or long, and each syllable must contain the vowel or diphthong plus the consonants that give it that particular sound. Let us look at the short vowel sound first.

Spelling rule #1: Closed syllables consist of a vowel followed by a consonant. They are almost always short vowels.

an/at/om/ic/al	*in/spec/tor*	*um/bil/ic/al*
em/bar/ras/sing	*op/pos/sum*	

In a closed syllable the vowel may be followed by two or more consonants and still retain the short vowel sound.

ack	*ick*	*uck*
ing	*end*	*ill*
odge	*edge*	*udge*

Note that these blends or digraphs form an essential part of the syllable and must remain with the vowel.

With double consonants, the division is between the two consonants unless they are at the end of the word. Never split a blend or digraph.

suc/cess	*ill/ness*
ac/cid/ent	*suck/ing*

When the letter *y* is in a closed syllable it should have the short *i* sound. When it is in an open syllable, it should have the long *e* or long *i* sound.

hymn	*gyp/sy*	*hap/py*	*ug/ly*	*ty/rant*	*fry*

When the *r* follows the vowel, it creates a unique sound which is very rarely a short vowel sound. This sometimes occurs with the letters *w* and *l*.

harm	*hernia*	*burn*	*down*	*palm*
torn	*firm*	*dawn*	*dew*	*hold*

Vowel diphthongs are almost always long vowels and are often in closed syllables, especially in single syllable words.

boat	*harm/full*	*boot*	*out/house*
bait	*sail/boat*	*seem*	*head/ache*

Spelling rule #2: An open syllable occurs when the vowel is not followed by a consonant. In most cases the vowel will then be long.

de/vi/a/tion	*cre/ate*	*si/lent*	*u/su/al/ly*
u/nique	*di/graph*	*re/main*	*a/ble*

Note that the letter *i* in an open syllable will usually have the long *e* sound.

pi/an/o	*mac/ar/o/ni*

Note that there are some unusual cases where a vowel diphthong produces a short vowel sound.

head	*thread*	*leather*	*sweat*	*plait*
bread	*dealt*	*health*	*dread*	*friend*
		cough	*rough*	

Note also that there are a few unusual cases where a closed syllable containing only one vowel does not produce a short vowel sound.

busy	*monk*	*many*	*won*

Spelling rule #1: Closed syllables consist of a vowel followed by a consonant.

The importance of correct syllabification *(syl/lab/if/ic/a/tion)* cannot be overemphasized. It is not only an important aide to correct spelling, but it also offers clues to the correct pronunciation. Invariably, poor spelling and poor pronunciation go together. Compare the following:

de/feat	*def/fer/rence*	*sil/ly*	*si/lent*
o/pen	*op/er/ate*	*ma/ting*	*mat/ter*
di/ning	*din/ner*	*ti/tan/ic*	*tit/u/lar*
pro/pel	*prop/er*		

ACCENTS

There are no hard and fast rules covering the placement of the accent. It depends a great deal on the origin of the word, its meaning, and whether it is a verb or a noun. With two-syllable words that are identical (homographs and heteronyms), the accent is placed on the first syllable if it is a noun, whereas the accent is on the second syllable when it is a verb.

NOUN	VERB	NOUN	VERB
the address	*to address*	*the refuse*	*to refuse*
the contract	*to contract*	*the entrance*	*to entrance*

With some words, the English prefer to place the accent on the first syllable, whereas North Americans place it on the second or even third syllable.

garage	*dictionary*

However, there are no clear rules, and so the student must use a good dictionary.

Spelling rule #2: An open syllable occurs when the vowel is not followed by a consonant.

CHAPTER 2
Vowels

$\mathcal{T}$raditionally, there are five vowels in English, but in practice we have six: *a, e, i, o, u,* and *y*. The letter *y* should be included among the vowels whenever possible because it is used as a vowel more often than it is used as a consonant. At times, the letter w acts as an auxiliary vowel when it replaces the letter *u*.

The *y* (or the Greek *i*, as it is called in Spanish) has two vowel sounds:

fly	*happy*	*dry*	*ugly*	*shy*	*slowly*

When the *y* follows a vowel, it helps form an important diphthong and does the work of the letter *i*.

bay	*bey*	*boy*	*buy*

All the vowels can make more than one vowel sound. There are about twenty different vowel sounds, and they can be spelled using over thirty vowel combinations. Often the same diphthong can be used to produce two, or even three, different vowel sounds.

A thousand years ago, almost all English vowels were short. The long vowel sound and the diphthong came, mostly, from imported and borrowed words. Today the majority of our words still contain these short vowels.

To avoid confusion, any vowel sound that is not clearly a short vowel sound should be called long.

pat	*pet*	*pit*	*pot*	*put*
ache	*eat*	*ice*	*open*	*use*

When teaching reading to very small children, we often use the old rhyme, "When two vowels go walking, the first does the talking." The child learns that the first of the two vowels in a diphthong will control the sound and almost always it will be a long vowel sound. Not all diphthongs follow this rule, but a very high percentage do.

aim	*eat*	*die*	*boat*	*true*
plain	*ceiling*	*pie*	*coat*	*suit*

CHAPTER 3

Vowel Plus r

*I*n English spelling, some consonants change the sound of the vowel that precedes them without using the silent *e*.

When the *r* follows a vowel, it almost always creates a new vowel sound and becomes the dominant consonant. Usually, there is a clear pattern, and the student will recognize it quickly. Often, however, the combination of vowel plus *r* can produce more than one sound. When we include diphthongs or the silent *e*, there are more than three dozen possible sounds.

The following are examples of a single vowel preceding an *r*.

| *bar* | *argument* | *arm* | *garter* | *ark* | *remark* |

In this group of words, the *ar* follows the letters *w* and *qu*:

| *war* | *quart* | *ward* | *wharf* | *warn* | *quarter* |

This group of words uses *er*:

| *mercy* | *were* | *berth* | *her* | *verse* | *clerk* |

This group of words uses *ir*:

| *bird* | *affirm* | *girl* | *dirt* | *third* | *first* |

This group of words uses or:

| *or* | *sword* | *for* | *north* | *born* | *mortal* |

In this group of words, the *or* follows the letter *w*:

| *word* | *worship* | *work* | *world* | *worm* | *worst* |

One anomaly is the word *worn*.

This group of words uses *ur*:

fur	*church*	*murder*	*burn*	*hurt*	*turkey*

One anomaly is the word *bury*, which is pronounced *berry*.

In *yr* words, when the *y* is followed by *r*, there are three possible sounds:

pyrite, gyrate	*pyramid, syringe*	*myrrh , myrtle*

CHAPTER 4

The Apostrophe

English is an extremely flexible language and has a number of advantages over most other languages. One of these advantages is the humble apostrophe. This tiny mark enables us to communicate faster and with less effort while still retaining clarity.

The apostrophe is used in the possessive and in contractions, and most native speakers would find it difficult to converse for even ten minutes without using a contraction, nor could they go half a day without using the possessive.

Many languages have no equivalent. For example in Spanish we must say "*the house of Mary,*" whereas in English we reduce these four words to only two and say "*Mary's house.*" Similarly, in most languages we must say "*I will not,*" but in English we reduce this to "*I won't.*"

Spelling rule #1: The possessive apostrophe indicates ownership. To use the possessive apostrophe simply add an apostrophe to the noun plus the letter s, then add the subject that is under discussion.

the president's speech	*Paul's dog*	*the dog's tail*

Words ending in *y* do not change the *y* to *i*.

the enemy's ships	*the monkey's tail*

Spelling rule #2: If the noun already ends in an *s* or if the noun is plural, the apostrophe is added after the *s*.

Charles' shirt	*James' car*
the ladies' dresses	*the elephants' feet*

If the plural noun is a special word, such as *women* or *children* or *mice*, then the rule applies and the apostrophe must be placed before the *s*.

the women's dresses	*the children's toys*

Pronouns such as *yours, ours, theirs,* and *its* do not use an apostrophe.

"Never use an apostrophe when a plural is intended."

8

Spelling rule #3: The apostrophe is never used with regular plurals.

cats	dogs	houses	dinosaurs

Note that there is often confusion between *it's* and *its*. The apostrophe indicates a contraction so *It is a nice day* becomes *It's a nice day*. The *its* without the apostrophe indicates possession: *The cat put its paw in its milk.*

If the object belongs to two or more persons, then the apostrophe and the *s* are used only with the final person mentioned.

Lily and John's house	*Mark, John, and Charles' boat*

The possessive apostrophe plus *s* should be no problem yet almost daily we can find examples of its misuse. Usually the error involves the plural. The rule is clear: *never use an apostrophe when a non-possessive plural is intended.*

CHAPTER 5

Contractions

"Ain't is never acceptable."

ontractions are as simple as they are useful. The apostrophe takes the place of a missing letter (or letters) and the two words are combined. In almost all cases, the first of the two words is not changed. The letters are dropped from the second word. Usually there is only one letter deleted, but there may be as many as four.

I do not	you will	it is	I am	Who would like coffee?
I don't	you'll	it's	I'm	Who'd like coffee?

The unusual contraction is *won't* for *will not*. Many years ago, it was *willn't*, but that is now archaic. There are a few other contractions that are now archaic, including *e'en* for *even*.

Sometimes a contraction may have two meanings:

We'd had a nice day but it began to rain.	we had
We'd all like a cup of coffee."	we would

There is one contraction that is frowned upon and never used by educated persons. This is *ain't*, which is the contraction for *am not*. The correct word, *amn't*, long ago fell into disuse and is now considered both awkward and archaic. Since there is no other contraction for *am not*, one would expect *ain't* to be quite acceptable. After all it has been around for over two hundred years. The main reason that *ain't* is not acceptable is that it has been, and still is, terribly overused and usually misused besides. It is often used in place of *haven't, hasn't, isn't, aren't,* and a number of other negative contractions.

English is a marvelously flexible language so if *ain't* is not acceptable and *amn't* is archaic, we can simply move the apostrophe to the preceding word and use *I'm not* instead. It would seem that this solves the problem, except that most contractions can be used in the interrogative—*haven't I? isn't it? don't I?* etc. Since we cannot use *amn't I?* we have to compromise with *aren't I?* or *am I not?* Because these seem awkward, however, whether we like it or not, the unacceptable *ain't* will probably be with us for many more years.

CHAPTER 6

The Silent e

*O*ne extremely useful feature of English spelling is the silent *e*. We place it at the end of a word in order to change the sound of the preceding vowel and thus create a new word. For example, *hat* becomes *hate, spin* becomes *spine,* etc. Not only does the silent *e* replace a vowel diphthong, but it also allows us to use vowel combinations to produce still other words, for example, *mete, meet, meat.* Unfortunately, we tend to overuse it, and sometimes there is confusion as to when to drop and when to retain the silent *e*. The basic spelling rules are quite simple.

Spelling rule #1: Retain the silent *e* when a consonant suffix is added:

| *like* | *likeness* | *love* | *lovely* | *waste* | *wasteful* |

Spelling rule #2: Drop the silent *e* when a vowel suffix is added:

| *like* | *likable* | *waste* | *wasting* | *love* | *lovable* |

Spelling rule #3: The soft and hard c and g rules must be observed. Therefore, words that end in a soft c or a soft g and are followed by a suffix that begins with a hard vowel or a consonant must retain the silent *e*.

| *change* | *changeable* | *nice* | *nicely* |
| *trace* | *traceable* | *age* | *ageless* |

Because of the large number of words that use the silent *e*, it is only to be expected that there might appear to be numerous exceptions and anomalies. Most of these apparent anomalies fit into patterns and obey the rules.

Spelling rule #4: The digraph *dg* is always considered soft, so the silent *e* is not needed when adding suffixes:

| *knowledgable* | *trudging* | *judgment* |

Spelling rule #5: There are very few commonly use English words that end in *u*; the ending is usually *ue*. In almost every

case, the silent *e* is dropped from these words when adding a suffix:

argue	*true*	*blue*	*sue*
argument	*truly*	*bluing*	*suing*

Spelling rule #6: The silent *e* is retained in words that end in *oe* when adding the suffix *ing*:

hoe	*toe*	*shoe*
hoeing	*toeing*	*shoeing*

Spelling rule #7: When adding the suffix *ing* to words ending in *ie*, we drop the *e* and change the *i* to *y* to avoid producing a double *i*:

tie	*die*	*vie*	*lie*
tying	*dying*	*vying*	*lying*

Note that at times, the pronunciation changes when a suffix is added and this causes a spelling change:

analyze	*line*	*prestige*
analysis	*lineage*	*prestigious*
conspire	*supreme*	*wise*
conspiracy	*supremacy*	*wisdom*

But there are some words that do not follow the rules:

whole	*singe*	*die*
wholly	*singeing*	*dying*
hole	*tinge*	*dye*
holey	*tingeing*	*dyeing*

Many problems can be traced to an understandable impulse to retain the silent *e* in order to protect the preceding vowel. When it is not obviously needed, the silent *e* should be dropped. The following words do not follow the rules:

acre	*fire*	*nine*	
acreage	*fiery*	*ninth*	
awe	*glue*	*cage*	*(compare stage*
awful	*gluey*	*cagey*	*and stagy)*

Note that *aweful* ("full of awe") and *awful* may now be considered two separate words with quite different meanings.

CHAPTER 7

The Letter v

The letter *v* may appear anywhere in a word except at the end. No commonly used English word ever ends in a *v*, and this explains a large inconsistency that students are quick to notice.

The silent *e* is used to modify the vowel that precedes it, but the silent *e* must be added to any word that should logically end in *v*. Therefore, we get *have* instead of *hav* and *active* instead of *activ*, and we spell *sleeve* with a superfluous *e*. There are many other examples.

From this point of view, the rule is illogical. But it does have the virtue of uniformity. Some of our spelling rules leave us with strange anomalies, but this rule is so simple that there are almost no exceptions.

rev	*to rev an engine, revolutions*
spiv	*a slang term.*
MIRV	*an acronym*

Note that one English word ends in a *v* sound but is spelled with an *f*. The word *of* is the only word ending in an *f* that has the soft *v* sound.

CHAPTER 8

Comparatives and Superlatives

$\mathcal{T}$he comparative words are not a major spelling problem. The only difficulty that students may encounter is when to double the consonant and when to leave it alone. The general rule for doubling consonants is covered in another chapter.

Spelling rule #1: The suffix *er* is used with single syllable words:

short	tall	fast	pink
shorter	taller	faster	pinker

When we are forming superlatives, the suffix *est* is used with single syllable words. The word must be preceded by *the*:

the biggest	the smallest	the youngest	the oldest

Spelling rule #2: Words of three or more syllables are preceded by *more* (comparative) and *the most* (superlative):

more beautiful	the most beautiful
more dangerous	the most dangerous
more difficult	the most difficult
more objectionable	the most objectionable

Spelling rule #3: With words of two syllables, one group uses *er* and *est*, but the others must use *more* and *the most*.

Adjectives that end in *y* simply change the *y* to *i* and add *er* or *est*:

dirty	jaunty	kindly	fruity
dirtier	jauntier	kindlier	fruitier
the dirtiest	the jauntiest	the kindliest	the fruitiest

Words ending in *ous* use *more* and *the most*:

anxious	callous
more anxious	more callous
the most anxious	the most callous

Words ending in *ful* use *more* and *the most*:

careful	dreadful	awful
more careful	more dreadful	more awful
the most careful	the most dreadful	the most awful

Words ending in *ing* use *more* and *the most*:

boring	loving
more boring	more loving
the most boring	the most loving

The English language contains thousands of adjectives of an extremely wide variety and many of them are regionalisms. When in doubt, it is best to use *more* and *the most*.

Note that one word that cannot be modified is *unique*. If something is unique, then it is the only one. There are no others. It cannot be *more unique* or *less unique* or even *most unique*. Either it is unique, or it is not.

Note that aweful ("full of awe") and awful may now be considered two separate words with quite different meanings.

CHAPTER 9

Plurals

*F*orming the plural in English is usually just a matter of adding an *s*. The interesting part of this rule is the number of exceptions to it.

English has always taken words and changed them, and the changes have almost always been toward a simpler spelling that fits the spelling rules.

Spelling rule #1: To form the plural of most nouns, simply add an *s*:

cats	dogs	houses	castles

Spelling rule #2: For words ending in *y*, if there is a vowel immediately before the *y*, then simply add the *s*:

boys	keys	subways

Spelling rule #3: If there is a consonant immediately before the *y*, change the *y* to *i* and add *es*:

monastery	sky	baby	pastry
monasteries	skies	babies	pastries

Spelling rule #4: If the word ends in one of the sibilants, such as *s*, *x*, *z*, *ch*, *tch*, *sh*, and *ss*, we usually add *es*:

fox	bus	mess	arch
foxes	buses	messes	arches
watch	bush	buzz	smash
watches	bushes	buzzes	smashes

Spelling rule #5: If the word ends in *f* or *fe*, we usually change the ending to *ves*:

calf	leaf	wolf	shelf	wife	knife
calves	leaves	wolves	shelves	wives	knives

Note that a number of words that end in *f* simply add an *s*:

chief	brief	safe	roof	cliff
chiefs	briefs	safes	roofs	cliffs
muff	oaf	skiff	toff	
muffs	oafs	skiffs	toffs	

Note that the plural of *staff* is *staffs* or *staves*, depending on the meaning.

Note that a few words may be spelled either way. These illustrate regional differences in pronunciation.

dwarfs or dwarves	*scarfs or scarves*
hoofs or hooves	*wharfs or wharves*

Spelling rule #6: If a word ends in *o*, we simply add an *s*:

cuckoos	*videos*	*banjos*	*pianos*

There are some exceptions to this rule. A few words that end in an *o* that is preceded by a consonant use the *es* ending. This special group of words is rapidly shrinking.

dominoes	*echoes*	*embargoes*	*potatoes*
Negroes	*vetoes*	*torpedoes*	*tomatoes*

There used to be three times as many words in this group, and some dictionaries still offer either spelling, but today, the preferred spelling is the simple *s*:

dominos	*mosquitos*	*salvos*	*tomatos*
cargos	*mangos*	*tornados*	*potatos*

Note that if the word is an abbreviation, we simply add an *s*:

kilos	*photos*	*hippos*

Spelling rule # 7: When forming plurals of hyphenated words, the general rule is to give the plural ending to the most important word, which is usually a noun.

mothers-in-law	*courts-martial*	*ladies-in-waiting*

Spelling rule #8: There are numerous irregular plurals:

foot	*goose*	*mouse*	*child*
feet	*geese*	*mice*	*children*
penny	*axis*	*tooth*	*ox*
pennies / pence	*axes*	*teeth*	*oxen*
	louse	*woman*	
	lice	*women*	

Note that *women*, *children*, and *oxen* date back a thousand years to the Anglo-Saxon.

Spelling rule #9: Some nouns are always singular. They have no plural form.

cod	sheep	pike	swine	aircraft
grouse	deer	fish	salmon	

Some nouns are always plural and have no singular form:

cattle	forceps	pincers
shears	scissors	series

And some words are neither singular nor plural, or perhaps they're both:

athletics	politics	mathematics
logistics	economics	gymnastics

English contains numerous foreign words that have not been anglicized, and their plurals are often spelled in different ways. But many of these are changing, sometimes right before our eyes. Our prickly friend the cactus, for example, may now be pluralized to *cactuses* instead of *cacti*, although most botanists prefer to use just *cactus* for both the singular and the plural. As for the poor old hippopotamus, in the herd, they are now *hippopotamuses* or, better still, just *hippos*.

The reduction of long, awkward words to short, clear abbreviations, such as *hippo*, is quite acceptable. For example, the piano was once called the *pianoforte*. Similarly gladioli or gladioluses are more commonly called *glads* and chrysanthemums are most often referred to as *mums*.

Of course, there are some who decry this modernizing of old and familiar words, but it fits the historic pattern. English has always taken words and changed them, and the changes have almost always been toward a simpler spelling that fits the spelling rules. In Italian, for example, the plural of *maestro* is *maestri*, but since we have borrowed the word, we give it the English plural, *maestros*.

Some words with irregular plurals may or may not be in the process of change. Only time will tell. Consider the following examples:

medium	*mediums*	*or*	*media*
formula	*formulas*	*or*	*formulae*
radius	*radiuses*	*or*	*radii*
appendix	*appendixes*	*or*	*appendices*
gateau	*gateaus*	*or*	*gateaux*
chateau	*chateaus*	*or*	*chateaux*
cello	*cellos*	*or*	*celli*
tempo	*tempos*	*or*	*tempi*

Note that the plural of *staff* is *staffs* or *staves*, depending on the meaning.

CHAPTER 10

The Past Tense

Note that one word that cannot be modified is unique. If something is unique, then it is the only one. There are no others. It cannot be more unique or less unique or even most unique. Either it is unique, or it is not.

*A*t one time or another, every teacher on playground duty has been confronted by a small child complaining, "He hitted me!" The child has learned the correct way to form the past tense of a verb, but, unfortunately, he or she chose the wrong verb. If the child had been pushed, punched, kicked, pulled, or shoved, there would be no problem. This illustrates the fact that, while we do indeed acquire most of the spelling rules by reading and writing, the formal teaching of spelling is still absolutely necessary.

The rule for forming the past tense of English verbs is quite simple and applies to most of the single syllable words in general use. It also applies to practically all the multi-syllable words.

Spelling rule #1: Add *ed* to the end of the word:

jumped	*acted*	*pushed*	*punched*
deliberated	*photographed*	*ventilated*	*disconnected*

Note that the ending *ed* is hardly ever pronounced clearly. Usually it is cut short, spoken very softly, or has a soft *t* sound. The clearest pronunciation will be at the end of a multi-syllable word like *consolidated, disconnected,* or *ventilated.* We need only listen to a Shakespearean play to realize that in the past most *ed* endings were pronounced much more clearly.

There is a small group of words that have a final sound closer to a *t* although they have the *ed* ending. Usually this *t* sound occurs after the letters *p* or *k*.

jumped	*hopped*	*limped*
clapped	*hoped*	*heaped*
looked	*poked*	*thanked*

Another group of words uses the *t* instead of the *ed* ending. The argument over whether to use the *t* or the *ed* ending is not new. Long before the advent of the printing press, writers used one or the other and sometimes both, often without any logical reason. The spelling reformers of the 19th century preferred the *t* ending because it suited their desire for phonetic spelling, but the *ed* ending poses no difficulties in either pronunciation or understanding, and by sticking to the rule we avoid yet another complication and retain uniformity.

Spelling rule #2: As a general rule, the *ed* ending should be used for the simple past tense. Verbs that end in *t* should be reserved for use as the past participle with the auxiliary verbs *have* and *had*.

Yesterday, I spilled the coffee.   *I have spilt the coffee.*

burn	burned	have burnt
dream	dreamed	have dreamt
learn	learned	have learnt
spill	spilled	have spilt
spoil	spoiled	have spoilt

The past tense of *sleep* was once *sleeped*, but that form has almost vanished in favor of *slept*. On the other hand, the past tense of *kill* is usually *killed*, but there are some regional dialects that use *kilt*. Similarly, the word *clapt* has given way to *clapped*. In card games, especially poker, the word *dealed* is often used instead of *dealt*. Although currently incorrect, it may one day be acceptable. Unfortunately, the correct past tense *shined* is moving in the opposite direction and the irregular *shone* is becoming more popular.

There is a small group of words that have no past tense.

cost	hit	put	set
cut	hurt	let	

The irregular past tense contains numerous interesting words, many of which have come down to us from the Anglo-Saxon and have suffered surprisingly little change over the centuries. They are short, basic, frequently used, single syllable words and they have a variety of endings. Clearly, many of these words were originally past participles, but over the years the regular past tense vanished and, as we no longer say *builded* or *spended*, the words have to serve as both past tense and past participle.

bend	bent	sit	sat	keep	kept
mean	meant	dig	dug	teach	taught
bind	bound	sleep	slept	know	knew
meet	met	feed	fed	tell	told
bleed	bled	slide	slid	lay	laid
read	read	feel	felt	think	thought
bring	brought	spend	spent	lead	led
say	said	fight	fought	win	won
build	built	stand	stood	leave	left
sell	sold	find	found	wind	wound
buy	bought	strike	struck	lend	lent
send	sent	have	had	wring	wrung
catch	caught	sweep	swept	lose	lost
shoot	shot	hold	held	make	made
deal	dealt	swing	swung	shine	shone

Note that the verb *to be* has its own unique rules, which are too complex for inclusion in this small book.

Past and *passed* are often confused and misused. *Passed* is a verb only, but *past* is an adjective that may also be used as a noun or even an adverb.

> *He passed me and then I passed him.*
> *It happened in the past year.*
> *In the past is when it happened.*
> *He went past me in a hurry.*

Note that *waked* is an acceptable past tense in place of the more popular *woke*, but both *awakened* and *awoke* are still in use.

In the present tense, we *hang* both things and people. In the past tense, *hanged* is reserved for criminals, while *hung* refers to suspended inanimate objects.

> *The picture was hung on the wall.*
> *The murderer was hanged.*

The currently incorrect past tense *shrinked* is often used in place of *shrunk*. It is interesting to note that when the past tense is used incorrectly, it is often a rejection of an irregularity and a clear preference for a version that follows the spelling rules.

Finally, please note that there is extraordinary confusion over *lie* and *lay*. Even the dictionaries agree to disagree. Perhaps it would help to bear in mind that "*chickens lay and people lie.*"

CHAPTER II

Prefixes and Suffixes

*T*he number of suffixes and prefixes (together called affixes) in the English language is truly astonishing. There are over fifty of Latin origin, over fifty of Greek origin, about a dozen of Anglo-Saxon origin, and a few from other languages, including Arabic.

These additions to the original root words are so common and so firmly entrenched in the language that often they are hard to recognize, as in the following common words. Which part of the word is the root, and which is the affix?

explode	*impolite*	*resign*	*innocent*
develop	*subject*	*support*	*alfalfa*

There are numerous more easily recognized prefixes and suffixes, and we use them enthusiastically wherever and whenever we can. The rules governing their use are quite simple.

The spelling rule is that the root word and the affix are not changed but simply linked.

recharge	*discharge*	*conserve*	*preserve*
uneaten	*eating*	*squashed*	*squashable*

Note that there are exceptions. There are times when the *y* must be changed to *i*:

happy	*happily*	*jolly*	*jolliest*	*envy*	*envious*

when the silent *e* must be dropped:

true	*truly*	*waste*	*wasting*	*fine*	*finest*

or the final consonant must be doubled:

fat	*fatter*	*thin*	*thinnest*	*cut*	*cutting*

These changes are explained in other chapters.

CHAPTER 12

Single or Double l

There are a number of prefixes and suffixes that contain a double *l*. For example:

all	*fill*	*till*	*will*
full	*skill*	*well*	

Although these affixes are quite common, there is often confusion as to when to retain the extra l. The spelling rule is quite simple:

In all but a very few cases, the second l is dropped.

Considering the many hundreds of words that include these prefixes and suffixes, it sometimes seems that they are never used with the double *l*. This is almost always true. Note, for example, that when *full*, *well*, and *all* are used as suffixes or prefixes. they are always spelled with only one *l*:

beautiful
welcome
alright (which is never used except informally)
fulsome
thoughtful
welfare
already (adverb; but all ready when everyone is ready)

At times it may look as if the double *l* is retained. This is not the case. When the suffix *ly* is added, the extra *l* is dropped so there are not three *l's* in a row:

beautifully	*peacefully*

Hyphenated words retain the double l:

full-length	*all-weather*	*well-off*
well-bred	*full-scale*	*all-paid*

Derivatives of a word must retain the double *l*:

full	*fuller*	*fullest*

Finally, please note that there is extraordinary confusion over lie and lay. Even the dictionaries agree to disagree. Perhaps it would help to bear in mind that "chickens lay and people lie."

Note that the word *fully* is the word *full* plus *ly* with the third *l* dropped. It therefore follows the rule.

While the charming old word *farewell* retains the double *l*, the equally ancient word *welcome* adheres to the rule and drops the second *l*. Interestingly, the word *fulfil* manages to drop the second *l* twice.

While the words *alright* and *all right* both follow the rules, the former is acceptable only in certain contexts.

The word *alone* comes from *all one* and follows the rules.

Note that the word *fill* is rarely used as a prefix or suffix. It is usually the root word, a derivative, or part of a compound:

filled	*filler*	*filling*	*landfill*	*refill*

With the words *skill*, *will*, and *till*, we come to a transitional stage. Some words have lost the extra *l* while others still retain it.

will	*goodwill*	*skill*	*skillful*
willing	*freewill*	*skills*	*skill-less*
willpower	*wilful*	*skilled*	*until*

While the rule is followed in British dictionaries, there are some American dictionaries that offer a choice of *skillful* or *skilful* and *fulfill* or *fulfil*. This is a fascinating reversal, considering how the British are so attached to the double *l* and Americans are not. When offered the choice, we should stick to the spelling rules and drop that extra *l*.

CHAPTER 13

Double the Consonant

One of the most irritating problems in English spelling is when to double the consonant and when not to double it. It is safe to say that even the best spellers are sometimes unsure and usually keep a dictionary handy. The double consonant almost always follows a short vowel, but a short vowel is not always followed by a double consonant. Most people would agree that the double consonant is an irritating anachronism which quite often is not needed.

Here is the spelling rule.

Double the final consonant only if the word ends in a single consonant preceded by a short vowel and the suffix is a vowel suffix. If it is a multi-syllable word, the accent must fall on the final syllable.

The following paragraphs are intended to clarify the rule.

The final consonant means just one consonant. If the word ends in *ch*, *sh*, or *ck*, then we do not double:

lunch	lunches	fish	fishing	back	backers

Single syllable words that end in *f*, *l*, *s*, and *z* are usually already doubled:

puff	puffing	kiss	kissed
small	smaller	buzz	buzzing

If an *s* follows *u*, then the *s* is not usually doubled:

chorus	chorusing	bus	bused

In most words that end in *x* and *y*, the letter is not doubled:

fix	fixed	toy	toyed

If there are two vowels, the consonant is not doubled. Almost always, the word has a long vowel sound:

feed	feeding	raid	raider	lead	leading

The combination *qu* is counted as one letter. Therefore the *u* is not considered to be an extra vowel:

quiz	*quizzed*	*quit*	*quitter*	*quip*	*quipped*

If the final *t* is silent, it is not doubled:

ricochet	*ricocheting*	*crochet*	*crocheting*

Note that the British pronounce the *t* at the end of *ricochet* and therefore correctly spell the participle *ricochetting*.

A suffix must begin with a vowel:

en	*ed*	*ing*	*ion*	*able*
er	*est*	*y*	*age*	*and so on.*

In multi-syllable words, the accent must be on the last syllable:

regret	*regretted*	*transmit*	*transmitter*	*forget*	*forgetting*

Occasionally there will be an accent shift when a suffix is added to a word. In these cases, the spelling rule must be followed. The words that fit the rule will double the consonant, but those that do not fit the rule will not:

prefer	*preferring*	*preference*	
confer	*conferring*	*conference*	
refer	*referring*	*reference*	*referee*
hide	*hiding*	*hidden*	

When adding *in* or *un* as prefixes, use only one *n* unless the word starts with an *n*:

numerable	*innumerable*	*necessary*	*unnecessary*

When adding *mis* or *dis* as a prefix, use only one *s* unless the word starts with an *s*:

agree	*disagree*	*satisfied*	*dissatisfied*
applied	*misapplied*	*spelt*	*misspelt*

When adding *ly* to a word that ends in *ic*, use *ally* (two *l*'s):

basic	*basically*	*tragic*	*tragically*
comic	*comically*	*frantic*	*frantically*

As a rule of thumb, when in doubt or when the dictionary offers a choice, do not double the consonant.

CHAPTER 14

Soft and Hard c

There are times when the *c* is soft, as in *city*, and other times when it is hard. as in *cat*. Understanding the rules that govern when the *c* is hard or soft will not only help alleviate some spelling difficulties, but it will also help in pronouncing words correctly. Understanding the rule is absolutely essential when changing the root word in any way, as when we are adding suffixes.

Spelling rule #1: The c is soft when it immediately precedes the letters *e, i,* and *y*:

cent	cinch	cycle	percent	precision

When adding a suffix that starts with *a, o, u,* or a consonant to a word that ends in *ce*, we must retain the silent *e* so that the *c* does not become hard.

service serviceable		notice noticeable

When adding a suffix that begins with *e, i,* or *y* to a word that ends in *ce*, we drop the silent *e* because it is not needed to keep the *c* soft:

service servicing		ice icicle

Note that there are about half a dozen scientific words that begin with the Greek syllable *coe* that do not follow the rule. In these words, the *coe* is pronounced *see:*

coelocanth	coelom	coelenteron

Spelling rule #2: The c is hard when it immediately precedes the letters *a, o,* and *u*:

car	come	curtain	cucumber	flacon

The *c* is hard if it is the final letter of a word or is followed by a consonant.

public	picnic	panic	climb	crumb	acre

Spelling rule #3: When adding a suffix that begins with *e*, *i*, or *y* to a word that ends in hard *c*, we must add *k* to keep the *c* hard:

panic	panicking	traffic	trafficking
mimic	mimicking	mosaic	mosaicking
picnic	picnicking	bivouac	bivouacking

Beware of anomalies:

arc	arced	arcing
zinc	zinced	zincing
disc	disced	discing

When two *c*'s are together, the rule still applies. The first *c* will be hard and the second will be hard or soft, depending on the letter that follows it.

accept	accident	eccentric	accord	accurate

Considering the extremely large number of words that use the letter *c* followed by one or more of the six vowels, it is astonishing that there are so few exceptions to the hard and soft rule. Note that one interesting problem is the word *Celt*. The ancient Celts did not have the letter *k*, so the name of their tribe should be pronounced *kelt*. It is sometimes spelled that way when it is used as a noun. The adjective *celtic* should be pronounced *keltic* following the pattern of the noun. The exception is Boston's basketball team.

CHAPTER 15

Combinations Using c

*T*he letter *c* is one of the most interesting letters in the alphabet. It has often been denounced as a useless letter that imitates *s* or *k*. However, when we look at it more closely, we find that it is not only one of the most often used letters, but it is also used in numerous quite fascinating ways.

The Anglo-Saxons pronounced it like a *k*, but, following the Norman French invasion and the later influx of countless Greek and Latin words, along with host of other foreign words, it began to acquire the extraordinary complexity that it now has. When the *c* has the *k* sound, the word is probably Anglo-Saxon in origin. When it has the *s* sound, it is probably French or Latin and arrived during the Renaissance. Centuries of usage have, however, caused quite a tangle. The *c* rules are not absolute.

When the *c* is followed by *h*, we usually expect the digraph sound produced by *ch*:

chapter	*cheese*	*chip*	*chocolate*	*chuckle*

But the *ch* may have the *sh* sound. These are mainly French words:

champagne	*Chablis*	*chiffon*	*machine*
chassis	*chenille*	*chute*	

And sometimes the *ch* may have the *k* sound. These are often Greek words:

stomach	*chorus*	*chemist*	*inchoate*
chord	*ache*	*chaos*	

Note that the only word to have a double *c* before the *h* is *saccharin*.

When followed by *k* in one-syllable words with a short-vowel, the *c* becomes silent:

sack	*stick*
clock	*check (which boasts both the ch and k sounds)*

Note that no commonly used English words begin with ck.

When the *c* is followed by *t*, it may sometimes be silent.

indict

When a *ci* or *ce* combination, appears, it may have the *sh* sound:

physician	*coercion*	*curvaceous*	*crustacean*
atrocious	*gracious*	*herbaceous*	*ocean*

When the *ce* combination has the *ch* sound, the word is usually of Italian origin:

cello   *concerto*

Note also that the *k* is rarely used before *l* or *r*, but it may be used before *le*.

clap	*crumb*	But:	*ankle*
creep	*climb*		*twinkle*
clue	*cross*		*buckle*

Again, there are a few exceptions, but they are also mainly exotic imports:

klutz	*klan*	*klaxon*	*kleptomaniac*
krill	*kraal*	*kryptonite*	

The *k* has to be used instead of *c* when a *k* sound is needed before the letters *e*, *i* and *y*:

kennel	*kestrel*	*keeper*
kill	*kindle*	*kymograph*

When a word needs a silent *e* at the end but also needs the hard *k* sound, the *c* cannot be used. We must use a *k*:

cake	*smoke*	*wake*	*broke*
like	*fluke*	*strike*	*duke*

After the letter *s* the *c* becomes silent if it is followed by *e* or *i*:

scene	*scent*	*crescent*
science	*scimitar*	*scissors*

But if the *sc* is followed by *a*, *o*, or *u*, it will sound like a *k*:

scare   *scone*   *scum*

And sometimes the *sc* digraph produces the *sh* sound when it is followed by the soft vowels, *e* or *i*:

conscience   *crescendo*   *luscious*

Chapter 16

Soft and Hard g

$\mathcal{M}$any writers lump the *c* and *g* together when explaining hard and soft sounds. Although they are similar in many ways, however, the *g* is more complex than the *c* and should be studied separately.

The ancient Celts did not have the letter k, so the name of their tribe should be pronounced kelt. It is sometimes spelled that way when it is used as a noun. The adjective celtic should be pronounced keltic following the pattern of the noun. The exception is Boston's basketball team.

Spelling rule #1: The *g* is soft before *y* and sounds like *j*:

gymnasium　　*gypsy*　　*gyrate*　　*biology* (or any other logy word)

Gynecology is the only exception. In North America, the initial *g* is hard. The second *g* follows the rules.

Spelling rule #2: When adding a suffix that starts with *a*, *o*, or *u*, or a consonant, to a word that ends in *ge*, we must retain the silent *e*. Otherwise, the *g* becomes hard.

manage　*manageable*　　*encourage*　*encouragement*

When adding a suffix that begins with *e*, *i*, or *y* to a word that ends in *ge*, we drop the silent *e* because it is not needed:

manage　*manager*　*managing*　　*encourage*　*encouraging*

English being the interesting language that it is, there are, of course, anomalies like *singeing*.

An interesting anomaly is the word *mortgage*. The variations, *mortgagee* and *mortgaged*, follow the spelling rules, but *mortgagor* breaks the rule by not retaining the softening *e*. It is nevertheless pronounced with the final soft *g*.

Spelling rule #3: The *g* is hard before *a*, *o*, *u* or a consonant:

gas　　*gone*　　*gun*　　*green*　　*glide*　　*ghost*

The *g* is always hard when it is the final letter in a word:

flag　　　*leg*　　　*rig*　　　*flog*　　　*drug*

The *ng* combination is often a problem. The hard *g* is pronounced softly but clearly. In words like *sing*, *singing*, *playing*, etc., it is pronounced so softly that it is barely audible.

clingy	stringy	springy

While the hard and soft rule is quite clear and logical, and it is valid for the vast majority of words, English being the wonderfully complex language it is gives us exceptions. These are discussed in the following paragraphs.

Spelling rule #4: Sometimes the *g* is hard before the letters *e* and *i*.

Hard ge words:

get	gear	geld	geyser
forget	finger	target	geiger

Hard gi words:

girl	giggle	forgive	gigabyte
gift	give	giddy	begin

Note that mathematicians and computer experts sometimes argue among themselves regarding the word *gigabyte*. Since it does not come from the English word *gigantic* but from the Greek word *gigas* ("*giant*"), it is properly pronounced with two hard *g*'s.

The words in this next group appear to be anomalies, but they actually form a special subgroup composed of single syllable words that end in *ing*. No other letter is added to keep the *g* hard, even though the suffixes start with *e*, *i*, or *y*.

dinging	dinger	dinged	bringing	bringer	
singing	singer		flinging	flinger	
pinging	pinger		slinging	slinger	
winging			stinging	stinger	
ringing	ringer		clinging	clinger	clingy
zinging	zinger	zingy	springing	springer	springy

Apart from this handful of semi-hard *ge* and *gi* words, there are no other exceptions among commonly used words.

Spelling rule #5: There are occasions when a word that ends in *g* must be followed by an *i* or an *e*. If it is a hard *g*, then confusion might arise because the *g* would become soft. In such cases a *u* is added between the *g* and the softening vowel.

The *gu* is used to keep the *g* hard, no matter what letter follows. A wide variety of words use the *gu*, which can be found at the beginning of a word, at the end, and sometimes in the middle.

BEGINNING	END		MIDDLE
guaranty	analogue	pedagogue	language
guard	fatigue	colleague	ambiguity
guerilla	vague	rogue	anguish
guess	demagogue	fugue	beguile
guest	vogue	morgue	sanguine
guide	monologue	synagogue	
guild	league	brogue	
guile	prologue	meringue	
guinea	epilogue	catalogue	
guise	dialogue	intrigue	
guitar	plague		

It is obvious that at least half a dozen words in the list above do not really need the *gu*. For example, the *a* in *guarantee* and in *guard* is not a soft vowel. Similarly, *league* and *colleague* do not need the *ue*.

However, some modernization has occurred. Over the past few years, many *ogue* words have lost the *ue* and now end with a simple *g*:

analog	demagog	epilog	monolog	dialog
pedagog	prolog	synagog	catalog	

CHAPTER 17

Changing the y to i

$\mathcal{H}$ere is one of those spelling rules that we all remember quite well, though we sometimes get a little confused when it comes to actually applying the rule and remembering the exceptions. The rules are quite simple and very logical and have few exceptions. The rule is applied when forming plurals and when adding suffixes.

Spelling rule #1: If there is a vowel before the *y*, add the *s* or the suffix:

boy	boys	day	days	play	player	playful

Spelling rule #2: If there is a consonant before the *y*, change the *y* to an *i* before adding the plural *es* or the suffix:

baby	babies	happy	happily	sloppy	sloppiness
cry	cried	sky	skies	merry	merrily

But if the suffix begins with an *i*, then the *y* has to remain or we would have a double *i* which is extremely rare in English:

pity	pitying	baby	babyish

When adding *ous*, most words change the *y* to *i*, but there is a large group that changes *y* to *e*. There appears to be no discernible reason for this anomaly.

victory	victorious	vary	various
injury	injurious	fury	furious
luxury	luxurious	mystery	mysterious
envy	envious		

But

pity	piteous	beauty	beauteous
plenty	plenteous	courtesy	courteous

Note that if the *y* has the long *i* sound, then it must be retained when adding *ly* or *ness* in order to keep the long *i* sound, even if it is preceded by a consonant:

sly	slyly	slyness	shy	shyly	shyness
dry	dryly	dryness	wry	wryly	

Words ending in *ay* usually obey the *ay-ai* spelling rule:

day	daily	slay	slain	pay	paid
gay	gaily	lay	laid, lain	say	said

Note that, apparently just to be contrary, the English language contains some words that sometimes reverse the process and change the *ie* to *y*. This apparent anomaly is necessary to avoid the occurrence of three vowels in a row, which is extremely rare in English.

die	dying	vie	vying	lie	lying	tie	tying

In the case of the word *money*, some dictionaries offer the choice of *moneys* or *monies* and *moneyed* or *monied*. Since the *y* is preceded by a vowel, there is no reason to change the *y* to *i* and thus no logical reason to break the rule.

CHAPTER 18

Using qu *Plus a Vowel*

*I*t is quite common to hear English spelling rules dismissed as either nonexistent or so riddled with exceptions that they are useless. This is not true. There is a large number of rules, but most of them are clear and logical, and most of them are valid rules. That is, they apply to such a high percentage of words in their particular category that there are few, if any, exceptions or anomalies. The *q* rule is valid one hundred percent of the time.

Spelling rule: In English spelling, the *q* may not stand alone. Excluding names, the *q* must always be followed by *u* and a vowel. There are no exceptions.

plaque	*quaint*	*queen*	*quick*	*quorum*
quality	*quest*	*quiet*	*quote*	*masquerade*

Note that our names are excluded because we may spell our names any way we wish. The names of foreign countries and cities, especially those that use a different alphabet, are often spelled with just a *q*:

Iraq	*Qiongshan*	*Aqaba*	*Qinghai*

A thousand years ago, the Anglo Saxons did not use the *q*. They used *cw*. Since there was no *k*, the *c* had a hard sound. *Cwen* is now *queen*. *Cwic* is now *quick*. The change in spelling occurred during the Norman French period, and today no commonly used English word begins with *cw*. The only such word in most dictionaries is a Welsh word, *cwm*, which is pronounced *kum*.

Note that although the *qu* produces the *kw* sound, there are only two words in most dictionaries that begin with *kw*, both recently borrowed words:

Kwanza	*Kwashiorkor*

And in North America, *cheque* is spelled *check*, despite the fact that the American Express Company sells traveler's *cheques*.

Note that mathematicians and computer experts sometimes argue among themselves regarding the word gigabyte. Since it does not come from the English word gigantic but from the Greek word gigas ("giant"), it is properly pronounced with two hard g's.

CHAPTER 19

The i Before e Rule

*T*here is one spelling rule that everybody remembers—at least the first two lines. Some of us can even remember the next line. But what about the fourth line?

In the case of the word money, some dictionaries offer the choice of moneys or monies and moneyed or monied. Since the y is preceded by a vowel, there is no reason to change the y to i and thus no logical reason to break the rule.

> *I before e*
> *except after c*
> *or when sounding like ay in neighbor and weigh*
> *or when sounding like eye in seismic and height*

There are so many hundreds of words that contain *ie* or *ei* that we cannot be blamed if we sometimes doubt the validity of this rule, but the fact is that the rule is valid for an astonishingly high percentage of words. The true anomalies are very few.

The spelling rule governs only those words where the two letters form a diphthong. They must produce just one sound. Hundreds of words contain these two letters but do not fit the rule because the letters form separate syllables.

Science is a two-syllable word.

Society has four syllables.

Quiet, *being*, and *deity* do not contain diphthongs.

In *hieroglyphics*, the letters *ie* form a diphthong, but in *hierarchy* they do not.

Spelling rule #1: I before *e*:

achieve	*hygiene*	*field*	*diesel*	*relieve*
believe	*chief*	*niece*	*grief*	*fief*

Note that there are hundreds of words in this group, but no commonly used English word starts with *ie*.

Most of the words in this group will have the long *e* sound, but there are exceptions:

sieve	*handkerchief*	*lieu*	*quotient*
friend	*mischief*	*view*	*patient*

Spelling rule #2. ... except after *c*:

ceiling	*deceit*	*receive*	*deceive*
conceit	*receipt*	*conceive*	*perceive*

A number of words seem to break this rule, but the vast majority of them are plurals like *vacancies* or comparatives like *juiciest*, where the *y* has been changed to an *i*. There are very few true anomalies.

ancient	*glacier*	*deficient*	*efficient*
species	*conscience*	*sufficient*	*proficient*

Even these few anomalies are subject to argument as to whether or not the letters form a diphthong. This depends on how the word is pronounced.

Spelling rule #3. ... or when sounding like *ay*. There are fewer than three dozen commonly used words that are spelled *ei* and sound like *ay*:

beige	*eight*	*weigh*	*chow mein*
geisha	*eighty*	*weight*	*feint*
peignoir	*eighteen*	*lei*	*skein*
surveillance	*inveigh*	*seine*	*freight*
deign	*reindeer*	*feign*	*obeisance*
heinous	*vein*	*neigh*	*sleigh*
reign	*inveigle*	*neighbor*	*dreidel*
veil	*rein*	*sheik*	

Some dictionaries offer an alternative pronunciation for three of these words. *geisha, obeisance,* and *sheik.* They are sometimes pronounced with the long *e* sound. but the long *a* sound follows the spelling rule and is therefore preferable.

Spelling rule #4. ... or when sounding like *eye*. There are slightly more than two dozen words that are spelled *ei* and sound like *eye*. Many of them have been borrowed from the German.

height	*heist*	*edelweiss*	*Pleistocene*
rottweiler	*seismic*	*eidetic*	*zeitgeist*
apartheid	*feisty*	*geiger counter*	*gneiss*
einsteinium	*kaleidoscope*	*stein*	*poltergeist*
Fahrenheit	*sleight*	*Gesundheit*	

Note that *either* and *neither* may be pronounced with the long *e* sound or the long *i* sound. Either pronunciation is quite acceptable on either side of the Atlantic. However, the *eye* sound conforms to the spelling rule therefore it is preferable.

The following words stick to the main spelling rule despite the fact that they have the *eye* sound:

die	*lie*	*vie*	*pie (and magpie)*
fie	*hie*	*tie*	*hieroglyphics*

There is a very small group of words that have the short *i* sound. Centuries ago, the word *foreign* was spelled *forein* and the word *forfeit* was spelled *forfet*. Here are additional words with the short *i* sound:

sovereign	*surfeit*	*counterfeit*

The following words are complete anomalies to the entire rule:

nonpareil	*weir*	*plebeian*	*codeine*	*heifer*	*seize*
their	*heir*	*protein*	*weird*	*caffeine*	*leisure*

Note that *lieutenant* is an interesting word. The British pronounce it *lef-tenant*, while the Americans pronounce it *loo-tenant*. The Latin root is *locum tenens*, a phrase that is still used by lawyers and which means a person acting for somebody else, an official representative. We still use the word *lieu* ("*in lieu of*"), which is pronounced *loo*. Therefore, the American pronunciation is historically more accurate and linguistically correct.

CHAPTER 20

Using k, ck, ic, ac

*T*o the student of English there must be times when the letters *c* and *k* appear to be interchangeable. Obviously they are not but we can not deny that there is some confusion. The Anglo-Saxons used the *c* when they needed a hard *k* sound and the *s* when they wanted a soft s sound, but the Normans introduced the *k*, which was soon followed by a flood of Latin and Greek words which often use the *c* when a hard *k* is called for. Add to this many hundreds of other imported words, and we have quite a mess. Over the years, however, spelling rules have emerged that serve to bring some order to the confusion.

Spelling rule #1: The *ck* is used immediately after a short vowel. Usually these are single-syllable words, but this group may include multi-syllable words when the syllable is closed or a suffix is added:

back	beckon	sick	mock
tracker	quickly	locket	pluck
peck	mimicking	stocking	luck

Note that no commonly used English words begin with *ck*.

Spelling rule #2: The *k* is used at the end of long vowel words and words that have a consonant after the vowel. This includes words that need a silent *e*:

book	soak	steak
poke	like	make
milk	sunk	bank

Spelling rule #3: Many words that derive from Latin or Greek use a *c* for the *k* sound after a short vowel, especially words that end in *ic* or *ac*. They are almost always multi-syllable word.

panic	picnic	traffic	public	tarmac
mimic	frolic	fanatic	domestic	bivouac

And in North America, *cheque* is spelled *check,* despite the fact that the American Express Company sells traveler's *cheques.*

41

Note that the anomalies are *arc* and *zinc*:

arc	*arced*	*arcing*	*zinc*	*zinced*	*zincing*

Fewer than fifty words end in *ac*. About half of them are descriptive nouns:

amnesiac	*pyromaniac*	*insomniac*	*aphrodisiac*

Only a tiny handful of words end in *oc*:

post hoc	*ad hoc*	*havoc*	*manioc*	*roc*

Note that the words *flack* and *flak* are not the same. The first refers to publicity, whereas the second is an acronym from the German words *Fleiger abwehr kanonen*, or anti-aircraft fire.

Visitors to Britain will find that *curb* is spelled *kerb*. Both words follow the spelling rules; both are therefore correct. Just to add to the confusion, in the last few decades many exotic new words using the *k* have been adopted and adapted into English.

anorak	*batik*	*beatnik*	*bolshevik*
musak	*polka*	*Sputnik*	*umiak*
vodka	*kayak*	*kulak*	*kopek*
kosher	*klutz*	*klan*	*krypton*

A historical note: Less than two hundred years ago, *public* and *domestic* were spelled *publick* and *domestick*.

CHAPTER 21

Using ch *and* tch

*H*undreds, perhaps even thousands, of English words contain the digraph *ch*. It can be used at the beginning, in the middle, or at the end of a word. The problem is when to use *ch* and when to use *tch*. The spelling rules are quite simple, and the anomalies number less than a dozen.

Spelling rule #1: The *tch* is used after a short vowel. It is used mainly in single syllable words, but when used in multi-syllable words, it will be part of a short vowel syllable:

batch	*ditch*	*notched*	*satchel*	*twitching*
fetch	*botch*	*hutch*	*wretched*	*crutches*

Note that no commonly used English word starts with *tch*.

Spelling rule #2: After a long vowel or a consonant, we usually use the simple *ch*:

each	*vouch*	*roach*	*mooch*
search	*bunch*	*porch*	*arch*

But there are anomalies:

rich	*detach*	*ostrich*	*duchess*
attach	*swatch*	*sandwich*	*which*
watch	*much*	*such*	*bachelor*

Note that both *breeches* and *britches* are correct, as each obeys the spelling rule.

Note that *lieutenant* is an interesting word. The British pronounce it *lef-tenant*, while the Americans pronounce it *loo-tenant*. The Latin root is *locum tenens*, a phrase that is still used by lawyers and which means a person acting for somebody else, an official representative. We still use the word *lieu* ("in lieu of"), which is pronounced *loo*. Therefore, the American pronunciation is historically more accurate and linguistically correct.

CHAPTER 22

Using j, ge, dge

$\mathcal{T}$he letter *j* is a very underused letter. About seventy-five percent of the time, when we hear the *j* sound it is actually spelled with *g* or *dge*.

Spelling rule #1: Except for a few exotic imports, the *j* is never used at the end of English words:

hadj	*raj*	*taj (as in Taj Mahal)*

The *j* can be followed by any of the vowels except *y*, but it is never followed by a consonant except in the popular contraction *Jr (junior)*.

Spelling rule # 2: We use *ge* when a *j* sound is needed at the end of a word if the word has a long vowel sound or if there is a consonant following the vowel:

cage, caged	*loge*	*huge*
range	*merge, merger*	*bulge*

Spelling rule #3: We use *dge* if the word is a short vowel word and there is no consonant following the vowel. There are many of these words. They are usually single-syllable words, but there are also a few multi-syllable words.

badge	*ridge*	*grudge*	*curmudgeon*
hedge	*dodge*	*knowledge*	*acknowledge*

When adding a suffix that begins with a hard vowel or a consonant, we would normally retain the final silent *e*, but when the *dge* is used, we drop the *e* because the *d* forms part of the soft *j* sound.

judge	*judgment*	*judgable*
lodge	*lodgment*	*lodgable*
abridge	*abridgment*	*abridgable*
acknowledge	*acknowledgment*	*acknowledgable*

Note that some dictionaries allow a choice when adding *able*, but there is no logical reason to retain the *e*. Compare *knowledgeable* and *knowledgable*.

Visitors to Britain will find that *curb* is spelled *kerb*. Both words follow the spelling rules; both are therefore correct.

CHAPTER 23

Using oy *and* oi

*W*hile the long vowel sounds produced by *oy* and *oi* are exactly the same, there is a logical reason to use one rather than the other. There are very few exceptions.

Spelling rule #1: The *oy* is used at the end of a word:

boy	*toy*	*deploy*	*employ*	*enjoy*

Spelling rule #2: The *oi* is used in the middle of a word:

spoil	*toil*	*loin*	*purloin*	*android*

Note that the *oi* must be followed by at least one consonant:

boil	*void*	*join*	*point*	*avoid*

Note that *oid* is also a suffix meaning "*resembling*" or "*like*":

asteroid (like a star)
spheroid (like a sphere)
android (resembling man or human)
planetoid (like a planet)

Very few words start with either *oy* or *oi*:

oil	*ointment*	*oink*	*oyster*

Note that many centuries ago, *oyster* was spelled *oistre*.

When adding suffixes, as the *y* is preceded by a vowel the *y* is not usually changed to an *i*.

boy	*boyish*	*enjoy*	*enjoying*	
employ	*employer*	*deploy*	*deployment*	
toy	*toying*	*annoy*	*annoyance*	*annoying*

Three words that retain the *y* in order to avoid the *oia* combination are *royal*, *loyal*, and *voyage*. The *oia* combination is very rare in English: *sequoia* and *paranoia*.

CHAPTER 24

Using ay and ai

*T*he long vowel sounds produced by *ay* and *ai* are exactly the same, but there is a logical reason to use one rather than the other. There are very few exceptions.

Spelling rule #1: The *ay* is used at the end of a word:

day	*say*	*delay*	*replay*

Spelling rule #2: The *ai* is used in the middle of a word:

main	*maim*	*wait*	*declaim*	*explain*

Note that the *ai* must be followed by at least one consonant:

raid	*plain*

There are very few words that start with *ay* or *ai*.

aid	*aim aimless aiming*
aigrette	*aye*
aide	*ayah*
aileron	*ayatollah*
ail ailing ailment	

When adding suffixes, as the *y* is preceded by a vowel, the *y* is not usually changed to an *i*.

say saying	*play player*	*pay payee*	*gay gayest*

Note that three words follow the rules when they take the past tense.

say said	*pay paid*	*lay laid*

Anomalies include the words *crayon*, *bayonet*, and *mayor*, which retain the *y* in order to avoid the triple vowel combination of *aio*. Many years ago, *mayor* was spelled *mair*.

CHAPTER 25

Using au *and* aw

These two syllables are similar in sound and could cause confusion. This is because the *w* in many of these words is being used in place of the *u* as an auxiliary vowel. But the spelling rules that govern *au* and *aw* are quite clear. They usually produce the *or* sound, as in *order, door, ball, raw*, but there are exceptions.

Spelling rule #1: The *au* spelling is used at the beginning or in the middle of a word. It is usually found in a closed syllable.

auction	audible	author
slaughter	applause	cause

The *au* spelling does not appear at the end of words except for a handful of exotic words which are mostly French and have an *o* sound or an *ow* sound.

bureau	plateau	beau	luau
trousseau	chateau	tableau	landau

Spelling rule #2: The *aw* spelling is used at the end of a word or syllable:

claw	saw	lawyer
draw	sawyer	rawhide

The *aw* spelling occasionally appears before a final *n* or *l*:

awl	yawl	spawn	bawl	prawn	crawl
brawn	yawn	drawl	drawn	sprawl	fawn
	trawl	lawn	shawl	sawn	

Exceptions are *bawd* and *bawdy*.

Note that many *aw* words were originally spelled with a *u*.

braule (brawl)	foun (fawn)	spraul (sprawl)
aul (awl)	launde (lawn)	poun (pawn)
scraule (scrawl)	baul (bawl)	tauny (tawny)

Note that *shawl* is from the Persian word *shal* and *yawl* is from the Dutch word *jol*.

Fewer than a dozen words begin with *aw*:

awe	*awesome*	*awl*
awed	*aweful*	*awn*
awful	*awkward*	*awning*

Note that *awe* is the only commonly used word in this group that uses the silent *e*.

Historical footnote: The ancient Celts used the *w* much as we use the *u*, and the spelling still exists in modern Welsh. For example, *cwm* is a word that means *a small valley*. Although *cwm* is the only word of its type left in our dictionaries, it is quite popular in Welsh place names, and its English variation, *combe*, is very common in England.

CHAPTER 26

Using ou *and* ow

Since the *ou* and *ow* combinations often make the same sound, it would seem that there is little difference between them. This is because, in many cases, the *w* is being used in place of the *u* as an auxiliary vowel.

Spelling rule #1: The *ou* spelling is almost always used in the middle of a word:

hour	shout	loud
compound	astound	boundary

Note that the *ou* is almost never used at the end of a word. There are very few exceptions.

you	bijou	thou
bayou	caribou	

There are barely half a dozen commonly used English words that begin with *ou*. One of these has a different sound.

our	out	ounce	ought (which
oust	ouch		sounds like aw)

Spelling rule #2: The *ow* is most often used at the end of a word.

cow	endow	how
allow	avow	bow

Only a tiny handful of commonly used English words begin with *ow*. Most of these have different sounds.

owe owed owing	own owner	owl

Note that the word *owl* was once spelled *oule*.

The spelling *ow* will occasionally appear in the middle of a word. The use of the *w* is sometimes necessary to prevent the occurrence of three consecutive vowels, as *ou* cannot be followed by a vowel, but *ow* can be followed by a vowel or a consonant. A large number of these apparent anomalies were once spelled with the letter *u*.

fowl	growl	dowdy	bower	town
chowder	powder	dowel	prowess	browse
vowel	towel	dowager	down	shower
howitzer	coward	howl	drowsy	
	gown	dowry	power	

Note these words that were once spelled with *ou* instead of our modern *ow*:

groule is now *growl*	*poudre* is now *powder*
goune is now *gown*	*doude* is now *dowdy*
houlen is now *howl*	*bour* is now *bower*
doune is now *down*	*shour* is now *shower*
toun is now *town*	*couard* is now *coward*

CHAPTER 27

Using oe, ow, oa

The long *o* sound can be spelled in a number of ways, for example, *throat, throne, though, throw, hoe, limbo*, etc.

Spelling rule #1: The most common spelling is the use of the silent *e* to modify the *o*.

home	phone	chose	abode	lone
stove	nose	bone	whole	stone
close	spoke	rose	hole	

In a smaller group are words that end in a simple *o*:

so	limbo	no	go	pro	echo
ago	also	hero	forgo	trio	fro

Another small group consists of those words that end in *oe*:

hoe	doe	toe	oboe	aloe
floe	roe	foe	woe	sloe

Spelling rule #2: The combination *ow* is usually used at the end of words. It does not change with suffixes or compounds.

tow	stow	mow	yellow	snowiest
snow	row	stowaway	borrowing	tomorrow
flow	crow	sparrow	below	bestow

One exception to the rule is *bowl*, which used to be spelled *boule*.

The only commonly used words that begin with *ow* are *own* and *owe* and their derivatives.

own	owner	owned	owning	ownership
owe	owed	owing		

Spelling rule #3: The combination *oa* is usually used in the middle of words:

moan	groan	float	broach	soak
road	toad	coast	goal	moat

Historical footnote:
The ancient Celts used the *w* much as we use the *u*, and the spelling still exists in modern Welsh. For example, *cwm* is a word that means a small valley. Although *cwm* is the only word of its type left in our dictionaries, it is quite popular in Welsh place names, and its English variation, *combe*, is very common in England.

51

There are very few commonly used words that begin with *oa*, and only one that ends with *oa*.

oaf	*oar*	*oak*	*cocoa*
oakum	*oat*	*oath*	

There are a few words that spell the long *o* as *ou*:

boulder	*though*	*soul*	*shoulder*

Note that there are also a few words that manage to produce the *o* sound in even more interesting ways:

sew	*broach*	*mauve*	*beau*

CHAPTER 28

Using or, ore, oar, our

*T*he *or* sound can be spelled in a number of ways, for example *for*, *fore*, and *four*, also *soar*, *war*, *wharf*, *ought*, *taut*, and *caught*. This variety of spellings should pose no problem because there is a pattern.

Spelling rule #1: By far the most popular of these spellings is the simple *or*. It is used at the beginning, in the middle, and at the end of words.

order	morning	sordid	furor
orphan	forbidden	adorn	neighbor
orthodox	deportment	terror	anchor

Spelling rule #2: The *ore* spelling is also extremely common. It is always used at the end of a word:

before	furore	tore	shore	wore
encore	foreword	galore	deplore	herbivore

Note that *furore* is the British spelling. Americans spell the word without the *e*: *furor*.

There is only one commonly used English word that begins with *ore*. It is *ore*.

Spelling rule #3: The *oa* spelling and the *ou* spellings are usually found in the middle of a word.

oar	aboard	boar	course	discourse
soar	hoard	roar	board	paramour
coarse	hoarse	four	gourd	court
board	hoar	source	pour	courtesan

Note that the *ou* spelling can produce a variety of sounds, for example *soup*, *source*, *sour*, and *journey*. Quite often, the pronunciation will vary from region to region.

Spelling rule #4: The *ar* spelling with the *or* sound is usually found after *w*, *wh*, and *qu*:

war	*warder*	*warning*
wharf	*reward*	*warp*
quarter	*quartz*	*quartet*

The spellings *aught* and *ought* can both be used to produce the *or* sound without the *r*.

bought	*brought*	*fought*	*aught*	*taught*
sought	*thought*	*wrought*	*naught*	*onslaught*
caught	*distraught*	*fraught*	*ought*	

A small group of words use the *au* spelling without the *gh* or the *r* to produce the same sound.

taut	*jaunt*	*taunt*	*jaundice*
taurine	*tautology*	*jaunty*	

CHAPTER 29

Using y, ee, i, ea ie, ey

There are seven different ways we can produce the long *ee* sound at the end of a word. This must seem rather excessive, but there is a pattern and there are surprisingly few anomalies.

Spelling rule #1: The most common way in which to produce the long *e* sound at the end of a word is by using the letter *y*:

ably	busily	diabolically	happy
academy	carefully	directory	oligarchy
bloody	chemistry	disability	prophecy
bogy	democracy	easy	very

Note that almost any word can be made into an adjective by the addition of the *y*:

handy	scary	bloody	jumpy
shorty	lowly	fatty	jittery

A small group of words that end in *y*, however, have the long *i* sound:

why	sly	fly	sky
prophesy*	occupy	multiply	decry

(*Note that this is the verb. The noun, prophecy, ends with the long e sound.)

When the *y* follows a vowel at the end of a word, it is usually taking the place of the letter *i*, and thus forms a diphthong. The *y* is usually silent or sounded very faintly.

day	buy	boy
toy	say	guy

When a word begins with a *y*, the letter is always a consonant. The exceptions are a few rare words like the archaic *yclept* and scientific words such as *ytrium oxide*.

When the *y* appears within a word, that word is most probably of Greek origin and may have the long *i* sound, the short *i* sound, or a combination:

Sometimes the sound is the same but the spelling differs. Take that famous alcoholic beverage. In the United States and Ireland, it is spelled whiskey, but the Canadians, the Scots, and the English spell it whisky. The original Scots Gaelic word was uisge, and the Irish Gaelic word was uisce. Just to make it more interesting, the Scots call it scotch, a word that they never, ever use to describe things Scottish.

hydroelectric	*pyromaniac*	*lyceum*
symphony	*physics*	*gypsy*

Spelling rule #2: Another way in which the long *e* sound can be spelled is with *ee*.

knee	*tree*	*whoopee*	*pedigree*
three	*flee*	*coffee*	*jubilee*
free	*agree*	*degree*	*chimpanzee*
bee	*decree*	*levee*	*filigree*

Fewer than one hundred commonly used English words end in *ee*. About half of them describe a person or a position:

licensee	*trainee*	*employee*	*appointee*	*promisee*
referee	*trustee*	*payee*	*detainee*	

Spelling rule #3: Another way to obtain the long *e* sound is to use the letter *i*. There are very few such words, and most of them are exotic imports, including many Italian words. The first seven words in this list are of course Italian.

confetti	*broccoli*	*graffiti*	*salami*
ravioli	*macaroni*	*spaghetti*	

safari	*ski*	*khaki*	*taxi*
ennui	*kiwi*	*tsunami*	*chili*
bikini	*sari*	*yeti*	
	yogi	*Nazi*	

Words containing the double *i* are extremely rare.

denarii	*skiing*	*radii*	*Hawaii*
genii	*alibiing*	*taxiing*	*Naziism*

Occasionally, some of these *i* or *ii* words will have the long *i* sound:

rabbi	*alumni*	*radii*
psi	*cacti*	*fungi*

Spelling rule #4: A very small group of words uses *ea* for the long *e* sound:

sea	*pea*	*lea*	*guinea*
tea	*flea*	*plea*	

Spelling rule #5. Only a few words end in *ie* with the long *e* sound:

laddie	boogie	goalie	zombie
aerie	bogie	coolie	rookie

Note that in the *ie* group we have a small subgroup of words that have the long *i* sound. They are mostly short, single-syllable words.

lie	pie	tie
die	vie	hie

Note that the *ie* or *y* is often added to a word to give it a casual or informal sound. Often it is a diminutive.

granny	sweetie	dinky	Billy
tummy	cutesy	Susie	Johnnie

Spelling rule #6: Another small group of words uses *ey* to form the long *e* sound:

key	kidney	donkey	gooey
bogey	jockey	money	trolley

Note that there is, however, a small group of words that have the *ey* spelling, but it is pronounced with the long *a* sound:

fey	whey	prey

Note that three words—*bogey*, *bogy*, and *bogie*—illustrate the amusing complexity of the words in this group. They are all pronounced the same, but one is a golfing term, the second a ghost, and the third a set of train wheels.

Sometimes the sound is the same but the spelling differs. Take that famous alcoholic beverage. In the United States and Ireland, it is spelled *whiskey*, but the Canadians, the Scots, and the English spell it *whisky*. The original Scots Gaelic word was *uisge*, and the Irish Gaelic word was *uisce*. Just to make it more interesting, the Scots call it *scotch*, a word that they never, ever use to describe things Scottish.

Historical note: In the overly quaint Ye Olde Tea Shoppe, the word *ye* was originally pronounced *the*. The *y* takes the place of an ancient letter called a *thorn*, now no longer used, that had the *th* sound. The word *yclept*, much loved by history buffs, is more properly *clept*, as the prefix *y* indicates the past participle only.

It is fascinating to review the variety of sounds that can be produced by the letter *y* alone or in combination. Take, for example, a word of French origin, *quay*. Usually, it is pronounced *key*, but in some regions it is called a *cay* and pronounced *kay*, while in still other parts it may be pronounced *kway*.

It is clear that the simple *y* is the logical ending for most of the words below. The *ey* and the *ie* endings are illogical but they are still used.

jockey	*lucky*
trolley	*holly*
goalie	*daily*

As our spelling slowly changes, there is a natural move towards a more logical spelling. The word *ecstasie* has long been replaced by *ecstasy*, and *horsey* is now commonly spelled *horsy*.

CHAPTER 30

Using u, ue, ew, oo, ou, etc.

*I*n English, the *oo* sound can be spelled in an astonishing number of ways, yet in nearly half of the eighteen samples given below, the letter *u* is not used, and in more than half of them the letter *o* is not used. In two of them, neither the *u* nor the *o* is used.

oo	do, too	ui	fruit	om	tomb
o+e	lose	u+e	rude	ough	through
du	duty	ou	you	wo	two
ue	true	oe	canoe		

To add to the confusion, there are two distinct ways to pronounce this popular sound. Many of these words have the simple *oo* sound that can be heard in *glue* and *too*. There are almost as many words that are pronounced with a distinct *yu* sound that can be heard in *beauty* and *view*:

few	feud	adieu	dual
duty	beauty	view	

Often this *yu* sound is a regionalism and must be respected when and where it is used, but it is gradually disappearing and words that were once pronounced with a *yu* sound are now often pronounced with the simple *oo* sound. A good example is the word *nuisance*. It may be *nyusance* or *noosance*. Obviously, there are many words that will always be pronounced with the *yu* sound.

feud	beauty	view
ewe	eunuch	curfew

Despite this plethora of possible spellings, there is a pattern to be seen and some general spelling rules can be found.

Spelling rule #1: An extremely large group of words uses the letter *u* to create the *oo* sound, sometimes with the silent *e* after the consonant, sometimes without it.

abuse	amuse	accumulate	ablution
allude	assume	ambulance	aluminum

There are about thirty words that start with the letter *u* and almost the same number end with it. The following list is a small, representative sample.

use	ubiquity	you
utility	fondu	menu

Spelling rule #2: The *ue* spelling is usually found at the end of a word:

blue	true	rescue
value	continue	virtue

Note that no commonly used English word starts with *ue*.

The *ue* rarely appears in the middle of a word unless it is used with *gu* or *qu*:

tongue	fatigued	croquet
rogue	conquer	delinquent

Spelling rule #3. The *ew* spelling is usually found at the end of a word:

few	new	blew
cashew	sinew	screw

Note that there are only two commonly used English words that start with *ew*.

ewe	ewer

The *ew* is not often found in the middle of a word.

jewel	pewter	skewer
sewage	shrewd	lewd

Spelling rule #4: The *oo* spelling is usually found in the middle of a word:

fool	choose	room
boot	bloom	groove

Note that the double *o* is quite rare at the beginning of a word, though there are some scientific words in this group.

oodles	ooze	oosphere
oomph	oophoritis	oomycete

There are barely a dozen words that have the double *o* at the end. About half of these are exotic words.

too	tattoo	shampoo
ballyhoo	kangaroo	igloo
bamboo	goo	taboo (also tabu)
zoo	cuckoo	

A single *o* may sometimes have the *oo* sound, with or without the silent *e*, but there are not many such words.

do	to	who	lose
undo	unto	whose	

Spelling rule #5: There is another very large group of words that uses the *ou* spelling to produce the *oo* sound. Excluding words that contain the suffix *ous*, we have about sixty words. However, many of these words are recently assimilated French words, or words of French origin that have not yet been anglicized.

souvenir	douche	bouquet	amour
silhouette	boulevard	velour	roulette
tourniquet	trousseau	pirouette	bivouac
	croupier	louver	

There are many other words in this group that may be considered fully assimilated, no matter their origin.

tour	ghoul	coup	coulee
detour	soup	recoup	routine
uncouth	group	rouge	through
youth	wound	coupon	
	route	acoustics	

Spelling rule #6: The *ou* is almost always used in the middle of a word. Few words start or finish with *ou*.

you	bayou	bijou
oubliette	ouzo	

Note that there a several other ways to produce the *oo* sound in English.

Many scientific words use the *oe* diphthong, but not always with the *oo* sound. For example, *onomatopoeia* or *coelacanth*. Which leaves us with just two words in this group—*canoe* and *shoe*.

The *eau* combination is used in only one word and its derivatives—*beauty, beautiful, beauteous, beautician.*

61

The *iew* combination is used in only one word and its derivatives—*view, interview, review, purview.*

The *ough* spelling with the *oo* sound is used in only one word and its derivative—*through* and *throughout.*

The *wo* group consists of just a tiny group of words.

two	wound	woo

In the *ieu* group, we have a very small group of words that are mostly of French origin:

purlieu	lieu	lieutenant
milieu	pre-dieu	adieu

An unusual but very ancient pair of words use the *om* spelling to achieve the *oo* sound—*tomb* and *womb.*

There is a very large group of words that use the *eu* spelling. Most of these are scientific words, but there are quite a number of words in general use:

rheumatism	pneumonia	eugenics	eucalyptus
eureka	pseudo	eulogy	deuce
neutral	sleuth	amateur	feud

A very small group of words uses *ui* to achieve the *oo* sound:.

bruise	cruise	sluice	suit
recruit	juice	fruit	

The *ua* group of words can be eliminated because *ua* is not a true diphthong; i.e., it is pronounced not as one syllable, but two. There are many words that contain this vowel combination, but in most cases the *al* is a suffix and when pronounced correctly, does not produce the *oo* sound.

dual	sexual	gradual	accrual	punctual
annual	actual	manual	habitual	

A note on pronunciation. There will always be differences of opinion regarding the correct pronunciation of the *oo* sound. With some words, it is clearly an *oo* sound, whereas with others the sound is closer to *uh*. Compare *wound* and *would*. This is a matter of personal preference and does not affect the spelling.

In review, we can see that the eighteen possible combinations can be reduced to a mere half dozen important spellings that group themselves into logical patterns.

62

CHAPTER 31

Using al, tial, cial, sial

Many nouns can be made into adjectives by the addition of the suffix *al*:

> *logical   herbal   coastal   additional*

Sometimes it is necessary to preserve or create a soft *s* sound before the *al*, so an *i* is inserted, resulting in either *cial* or *tial*. There are about seventy commonly used words that employ one of these endings. Because they sound more or less, the same, the problem is which one to use.

Spelling rule #1: The vast majority of words in this group will end in *tial*. This includes all words coming from a root that ends in *t*:

> *torrential   differential   tangential*
> *presidential   penitential*

Spelling rule #2: Words that come from a root that ends in a soft *c* or an *x* will use the *cial* ending:

> *commercial   official   provincial   crucial*
> *racial   facial   social*

Spelling rule #3: A major exception is any word that comes from a root that ends in *ence* or *ance*. These will use *tial*:

> *sequential   confidential   residential   essential*
> *substantial   circumstantial insubstantial preferential*

Anomalies include *equinoctial*, *palatial*, and *axial*.

Note that only two commonly used English words use the highly logical *sial* ending: *ambrosial* and *controversial*.

Note also that some dictionaries offer a choice between *spacial* and *spatial*. Obviously, the correct spelling should be *spacial*. Similarly, the adjective *palatial* makes absolutely no sense, but the logical *palacial* has not yet appeared in our dictionaries.

Historical footnote:
In the overly quaint Ye Olde Tea Shoppe, the word *ye* was originally pronounced *the*. The *y* takes the place of an ancient letter called a thorn, now no longer used, that had the *th* sound. The word *yclept*, much loved by history buffs, is more properly *clept*, as the prefix *y* indicates the past participle only.

CHAPTER 32

Using efy and ify

*T*he endings *efy* and *ify* are not a difficult problem because there are only three anomalies. The verb suffix *fy* means "*to make or to become,*" and there are about one hundred words that use this suffix, which comes from the Latin *facere,* meaning "*to make.*" *Solidify,* for example, means "*to make solid.*"

Spelling rule #1: The ending *ify* is used with almost all the words in this group:

dignify	solidify	terrify	liquify
amplify	identify	testify	rarify

Spelling rule #2: The ending *efy* is used with only three words and their derivatives:

putrefy	putrefying	putrefaction
stupefy	stupefied	stupefyingly
tumefy	tumefying	tumefaction

Until quite recently, *liquify* and *rarify* were spelled with an *e.* Three *efy* words come from Latin roots that contain the letter *e*: *liquere, putrere,* and *stupere,* but *rarify* comes from *rarus,* which does not contain an *e.* The modern spelling is therefore correct. In time the other words will follow suit and exchange the *e* for an *i.*

Naturally, there are many other words that end in *fy* but do not contain this *ify* suffix. They often have the long *e* sound, but there are other vowel sounds, too:

leafy	beefy	goofy	fluffy

CHAPTER 33

Using cede, sede, ceed, seed

$\mathcal{A}$lthough there is only a small handful of commonly used English words that use one of these endings, despite their small numbers, they can cause a great deal of irritation. This takes a little explanation. *Supersede* comes from the Latin *sedere*, meaning *"to sit,"* whereas most of the other words come from *ceder*, *"to go ahead."* Unfortunately, over the centuries, the spelling has gotten slightly mixed so that we now have some words spelled with *ee*.

Spelling rule #1: The spelling *seed* is only used for *seed*, including its compounds and derivatives:

seed	seeding	reseed	seedlings	poppy seed	apple seed

Spelling rule #2: Almost all the other words use *cede* (from *ceder*):

cede	recede	antecede	concede
secede	accede	intercede	precede

Spelling rule #3: There are two other possible endings, *eed* and *ede*:

exceed	exceeding	succeed	succeeding
proceed	proceeding	supersede	

Note that *supersede* is the only commonly used word in the English language to use *sede*.

When the long *e* sound is changed to a short *e* sound, it will be spelled with only one *e*—*succeed, success, intercede, intercession*. One curiosity is *proceed*, which loses the double *e* when it becomes *procedure* but retains the long *e* sound.

The word *emceed* is the past tense of *emcee*, which is formed from an acronym (MC, *Master of Ceremonies*) and is so new that some writers prefer not to use it.

CHAPTER 34

Using er, or, ar, re, our

These five endings should pose no problem. This is because we use only three of them. Two hundred years ago, Noah Webster eliminated both the *re* and the *our* from American English and simplified the whole matter. The British still cling to numerous words spelled with the imitation French *our* ending—*colour, labour, honour, neighbour.* In the U.S. we have only a handful—compare *hour, four, tour.*

our	*contour*	*your*	*devour*	*sour*
flour	*dour*	*detour*	*pour*	*tour*
four	*scour*	*hour*	*velour*	

The *re* ending also illustrates a difference between British and American spelling. On the other side of the Atlantic, they spell about three dozen words with the *r* before the *e*—*millimetre, centre, theatre,* etc.. In the U.S., we have reduced it to fewer than half a dozen commonly used words that are spelled with the *re* only so that they will conform to the soft and hard *c* and *g* rules:

acre	*lucre*	*massacre*	*mediocre*	*ogre*

Spelling rule #1: The *er* ending is used for occupations or for persons who carry out an action:

butcher	*writer*	*eater*	*teacher*
lawyer	*baker*	*jumper*	*drinker*
driver	*banker*	*maker*	*porter*

Spelling rule #2: The *or* ending is used with root words that end in *t* or *s*:

actor	*editor*	*doctor*	*successor*	*supervisor*
visitor	*collector*	*professor*	*sponsor*	

During the 18th century, there was a period when French spellings were fashionable and a number of words were spelled with either *or* or *our*:

governor	ambassador	councilor	survivor	jailor
counselor	surveyor	chancellor	conqueror	author

Note that words with a soft *c* or a soft *g* will naturally need the *er* ending to retain the correct sound:

grocer	officer	manager	passenger

If the word ends in a silent *e*, it will usually take the *er* ending:

bake	baker	write	writer
hike	hiker	smoke	smoker

Comparative adjectives usually end in *er*.

larger	smaller	better
bigger	taller	shorter

Spelling rule #3: The vast majority of words ending in *ar* are adjectives:

familiar	particular	circular
triangular	regular	modular

However, there are about sixty nouns that also end in *ar*:

dollar	nectar	grammar	funicular	seminar
beggar	calendar	quasar	molar	

Note that sometimes the different spelling indicates a different meaning:

A *sailer* is a type of ship, but a *sailor* is a seaman.

A *censer* is for burning incense, but a *censor* is a person.

A *quitter* is a person who quits, but *quittor* is a horse disease.

Lumber refers to wood, but *lumbar* refers to the spine.

Note that *finger* is an anomaly because the *er* is part of the root word. It also breaks the hard *g* rule.

Some dictionaries offer *adviser* or *advisor*, also *conjurer* or *conjuror*. As these persons are carrying out an action, the ending should be *er*.

Chapter 35

Using y, ry, ary, ery, iry, ory, ury, yry

To the student of English, these seven possible endings must seem enormously confusing. But they do fit into logical patterns. Almost all of these endings are simply variations of the *ry* suffix.

Spelling rule #1: Most words in this group simply use the root word followed by *ry*. If the word ends in *r*, do not double the *r*:

burglary	flowery	wintery	predatory	watery
blistery	floury	summery	rectory	rubbery
	armory	hairy	silvery	

Spelling rule #2: The silent *e* is often dropped:

inquire	inquiry	treasure	treasury	mire	miry
wire	wiry	injure	injury		

And the vowel before the *ry* is often dropped:

ancestor	ancestry	anger	angry	register	registry
enter	entry	barometer	barometry	hunger	hungry

Note that most of the words that end in *ary* are adjectives.

temporary	fragmentary	imaginary	auxiliary
necessary	solitary	rudimentary	

But the nouns in the *ary* group are usually complete words:.

library	rosary	secretary
commissary	notary	dictionary

Spelling rule #3: Most of the words that end in *ery* are nouns that often describe either an occupation or an action:

archery	hatchery	surgery
adultery	lechery	thievery
brewery	sorcery	treachery

The word emceed is the past tense of emcee, which is formed from an acronym (MC, Master of Ceremonies) and is so new that some writers prefer not to use it.

Note that there are adjectives in the *ery* group, but they are there because the root word ends in *er*:

water watery	blister blistery	winter wintery
copper coppery	flower flowery	twitter twittery
silver silvery	rubber rubbery	

Words that end in *ory* are fairly evenly divided between nouns and adjectives. Most *ory* endings follow an *s* or a *t*:

advisory	expository	supervisory	sensory
accessory	promissory	valedictory	laboratory

There are many words that end in *ry* where the *ry* is not a suffix:

ivory	theory	mystery	glory
memory	rosary	allegory	history

There are only a few commonly used words that end in *ury*.

perjury	century	usury	treasury
injury	luxury	floury	mercury

Even fewer commonly used words end in *iry*:

airy	wiry	hairy	miry
fairy	inquiry	dairy	

And only two words use the *yry* spelling—*porphyry* and *eyry*. There are four ways to spell this rare word—*eyry*, *eyrie*, *aery*, and *aerie*.

There are only about thirty words that use the double *r*, which occurs mostly after a short vowel:

carry	berry	lorry	flurry
marry	cherry	sorry	slurry

English is a constantly changing language, and it is possible that eventually most of the words in this group will end in the simple *ry*. The archaic *jewellery* is already spelled *jewelry*, and *wintery* is gradually being replaced by *wintry*. Perhaps we may one day lose the surplus *e* in *tomfoolery*.

CHAPTER 36

Using ly, ally, ely, ily, lly, uly

T he suffix *ly* is used to change an adjective into an adverb. There are a half dozen different ways to do this, and there is a reason for each one. The rules are clear. There are few anomalies.

Spelling rule #1: In the vast majority of cases, we simply add *ly* to the root word:

quickly	softly	kindly	firmly
slowly	perfectly	coldly	astonishingly

If the root word ends in *l* or if it has the suffix *ful*, we retain the *l* when we add *ly*. It will seem to have doubled the *l*, but this is not a double *l*. It just looks like it.

annually	finally	beautifully
infinitesimally	gracefully	formally

Spelling rule #2: If the root word ends in *al*, then the suffix must be *ally*:

finally	royally	annually
dismally	formally	critically

Spelling rule #3: Words ending in *ic* always use *ally* to retain the hard *c*. There are many words in this group:

academically	dramatically	artistically	frantically
mechanically	automatically	organically	cynically

The anomaly is *public*, which becomes *publicly*.

Spelling rule #4: In most cases the silent *e* is retained:

leisurely	desperately	impassively	fortunately
closely	finely	sensitively	widely

But some commonly used words drop the silent *e*:

wholly	duly	only	truly

Words ending in *le* simply change the *e* to a *y*:

terribly   subtly   horribly

Spelling rule #5: Change the *y* to *i* before adding the suffix:

happily   prettily   dizzily   bloodily
funnily   ordinarily   nastily

But there is a small group of single-syllable words that do not change the *y* to *i*:

coyly   dryly   feyly   wryly
shyly   slyly   spryly

CHAPTER 37

Using able *and* ible

*T*he spelling rules governing the suffixes *able* and *ible* are quite simple if we bear in mind that *ible* is a variant of *able* and is used in only a few cases. These suffixes are mainly used to create adjectives, and there are hundreds of them. When new words are coined, they usually use *able*. When one of these words is changed into another form, the pattern does not change, so we may treat them as a single group.

VERB	ADJECTIVE	ADVERB	NOUN
rely	reliable	reliably	reliability
depend	dependable	dependably	dependability
envision	visible	visibly	visibility

Spelling rule #1: Add *able* to the whole root word:

avoid	avoidable	accept	acceptable
break	breakable	wash	washable
eat	eatable	reason	reasonable
drink	drinkable	fix	fixable

Spelling rule #2: If the root does not appear to be a complete word, it will probably take ible:

audible	edible	indelible	ostensible
credible	fallible	negligible	legible

Spelling rule #3: A large number of root words that end in *s* or *t* use the *ible* ending. Also, words ending in a soft *c* or a soft *g* will also usually use the *ible* ending.

sensible	accessible	reversible	collapsible
constructible	contemptible	exhaustible	convertible
forcible	irascible	illegible	tangible

Spelling rule #4: Words ending in a silent *e* usually drop the silent *e* when adding *able* or *ible*, especially when it follows a soft *c* or soft *g*:

admirable	reducible	debatable	submergible
consolable	defensible	sensible	forgivable

Note that there is no commonly used English word that ends in *eible*.

Spelling rule #5: If the root ends in a soft *c* or a soft *g*, it must retain the silent *e* if the suffix is *able*:

noticeable	bridgeable	peaceable	changeable
manageable	useable	salvageable	likeable

But in order to retain the correct sound, a small group of words do not lose the silent *e*:

agreeable	impermeable	decreeable
permeable	fireable	tapeable

If the root word ends in *i* or in a *y* which will change to an *i*, the suffix cannot be *ible*, as we would then have a double *i*. We must use *able*.

variable	enviable	reliable	certifiable

Spelling rule #6: If the root word ends in a hard *c* or a hard *g*, it must be followed by *able* to preserve the sound of the consonant:

implacable	indefatigable	despicable	navigable

Words ending in *x* take *able*, with one exception.

taxable	relaxable	mixable	fixable

The exception is *flexible*. There seems to be no logical reason for this exception, so let's just say that English is a *flexible* language.

Continuity is essential when forming derivatives. If the root word can accept the suffix *ate* or *ation*, then it must use *able*:

demonstrate	demonstration	demonstrable
tolerate	toleration	tolerable
tax	taxation	taxable
impregnate	impregnation	impregnable

To retain continuity when forming derivatives, if the root can accept *ion* but not *ation*, then we must use *ible*:

audit	audition	audible
combust	combustion	combustible
collect	collection	collectible
corrupt	corruption	corruptible

CHAPTER 38

Using ous, ious, eous, uous

T he suffix *ous*, which means *"full of or like,"* is used to create adjectives. There are many of these words, but the rules governing the use of the suffix are simple and logical. Over time, many of the root words have disappeared completely or only a portion of the root word remains, but we still have the adjective.

Spelling rule #1: In the majority of cases, the *ous* is added to the root word or a portion of the root word. Almost always, if the root ends in a consonant it will take the simple *ous*:

danger	dangerous	hazard	hazardous
marvel	marvelous	odor	odorous
cancer	cancerous		

Spelling rule #2: If the root word ends in a silent *e*, then, in most cases, the *e* is dropped.

nerve	nervous	ridicule	ridiculous
fame	famous	adventure	adventurous
desire	desirous	torture	torturous
blaspheme	blasphemous		

Spelling rule #3: If the root word ends in a soft *g* followed by a silent *e*, then the *e* is retained to protect the *g* but it is still silent:

advantage	advantageous	rampage	rampageous
courage	courageous	umbrage	umbrageous
outrage	outrageous		

Spelling rule #4: If the root ends in a soft *c* followed by a silent *e*, then the *e* is changed to *i* and has the *sh* sound:

grace	gracious	vice	vicious
malice	malicious	space	spacious
office	officious	avarice	avaricious

Spelling rule #5: If the root ends in *y*, we change the *y* to *i* and the new word will have the long *e* sound:

envy	envious	vary	various
harmony	harmonious	fury	furious
mystery	mysterious	luxury	luxurious

Note these two anomalies—*piteous* and *beauteous*. The *eous* is pronounced as two syllables, *e-ous*.

If the root ends in *c*, *t*, or *x*, then the suffix will be *ious* and it will have a *sh* sound. While many of the root words have disappeared, we still have the adjectives.

conscious	delicious	anxious
obnoxious	ambitious	cautious

If the root ends in *u*, the *u* is retained and is always pronounced clearly:

fatuous	virtuous	voluptuous
impetuous	arduous	conspicuous

In the largest group of *ious* words, the *i* is always pronounced clearly and with the long e sound:

bilious	vicarious	serious
hilarious	curious	sanctimonious

If the root ends in an *f*, it will change to a *v*. There are only two commonly used words in this group—*grievous* and *mischievous* (which has only three syllables, not four).

Up to this point the spelling rules for the *ous* words are clear and logical, but there are at least fifty commonly used English words that have the *eous* ending, even though the *e* is not protecting a soft *g* and is clearly pronounced. Logically, most of these words should use an *i*. But they do not.

hideous	spontaneous	instantaneous	extraneous
miscellaneous	erroneous	righteous	bounteous
	gaseous	nauseous	

CHAPTER 39

Using tion, sion, ssion, tian, cian, cion, shion, xion, sian, cean

T he *tion* ending, in all its variations, is usually used to turn a verb into a noun. There are hundreds of examples. This "*shun*" ending can be produced in about ten different ways. If this seems rather excessive, there is a logical pattern. Interestingly, there is no commonly used English word that uses *shun* as an ending, apart from the word *shun*.

Spelling rule #1: By far the majority of words in this category will use the *tion* ending:

attention	*reflection*	*invention*
imitation	*assimilation*	*fraction*

Spelling rule #2: The suffix *sion* is a variation of *tion* and is usually used after roots ending in *d*, *s* with a silent *e*, and sometimes *t*:

pretend	*pretension*	*converse*	*conversion*
comprehend	*comprehension*	*convulse*	*convulsion*
profuse	*profusion*	*avert*	*aversion*

Words ending in double *s* will be spelled *ssion*:

confess	*confession*	*access*	*accession*
possess	*possession*	*express*	*expression*

Words ending in *mit* will also use the double *s*:

remit	*remission*	*permit*	*permission*
admit	*admission*	*commit*	*commission*

Words ending in *cede* and *ceed* also use the double *s*:

secede	*secession*	*proceed*	*procession*
accede	*accession*	*concede*	*concession*

Spelling rule #3: The *cian* ending is almost always used to indicate a trade, skill, or a profession:

optician	*mortician*	*musician*
beautician	*physician*	*magician*

The *tian* ending is similar to *cian*, but usually indicates a place of origin or a belief:

Martian	*Dalmatian*	*Christian*	*Faustian*

Note that sometimes these suffixes appear to be interchangeable, but they are not. They may have to be spelled with a *c* or an *s* or another consonant, depending on the root word.

Thracian	*Joycean*	*Asian*	*Philadelphian*

Fewer than half a dozen words use *xion*. Some writers still insist on *inflexion* and *genuflexion* instead of *inflection* and *genuflection*, but these are archaic forms. There are only five words remaining, and one of these is slowly changing. *Complexion* is becoming *complection*.

crucifixion	*suffixion*	*transfixion*	*effluxion*

There is also a very small group of words with other endings:

ocean	*suspicion*	*fashion*
cushion	*cetacean*	*coercion*

Considering the hundreds of words that use the *shun* ending, it is truly astonishing how many of them fit neatly into the spelling rules and how very few are anomalies.

Chapter 40

Using le, el, al, il, ol, ul, yl

*W*hen we consider that all these endings make more or less the same sound, this is an extraordinary range of possibilities. A careful look will show that there are quite valid reasons and there is a pattern to it all. It is obvious that poor pronunciation often leads to confusion between these endings. The *al* suffix, for example, can be easily distinguished if it is clearly pronounced, but the *el* suffix is all too often slurred into a *le* or a schwa sound. The three most common endings are *le*, *el*, and *al*. The problem is simplified if we bear in mind the difference between an *angel* and an *angle*.

Spelling rule #1: If the root ends in a soft *c* or a soft *g*, it cannot be followed by *le* or *al*, it must therefore use *el*:

cancel	*parcel*	*excel*	*angel*	*cudgel*

Spelling rule #2: If the ending follows a hard *c* or a hard *g*, it cannot be *el* and must therefore be either *le* or *al*:

magical	*chemical*	*struggle*	*vehicle*
miracle	*angle*	*jingle*	*regal*
musical	*frugal*	*prodigal*	

Spelling rule #3: The vast majority of words ending in *al* are adjectives:

horizontal	*suicidal*	*universal*
tidal	*vertical*	*musical*
medical	*colossal*	*chemical*

Note that words ending in the silent *e* will lose the *e* before the *al*:

brutal	*tidal*	*universal*	*suicidal*

Spelling rule #4: A large majority of words ending in *cle* or *ckle* are nouns:

miracle	*tentacle*	*article*	*buckle*
barnacle	*testicle*	*particle*	*cockle*
monocle	*vehicle*	*icicle*	*freckle*

In English spelling, the *le* never follows the letters *m, n, r, v,* and *w*. Only six words use *sle*:

isle	*lisle*	*tussle*
aisle	*hassle*	*tousle*

The following consonants are usually followed by *le*: *b, d, f, g, p,* and *z*. There are a few exceptions:
The letter *t* may be followed by *le, el,* or *al*:

beetle	*hotel*	*coastal*
mantle	*pastel*	*total*

The *yl* ending is found mainly on scientific words such as *pterodactyl* and *chlorophyl*, leaving us with only two commonly used words—*sibyl* and *idyl*.

Very few words end in *ul*. If we exclude almost two hundred words that end in *ful* (*useful, beautiful,* etc.) and words containing the diphthongs *au* and *ou* (*haul, maul, ghoul, foul,* etc.), we are left with only four *ul* words:

annul	*consul*	*ampul*	*mogul*

Words ending in *ol* are also quite rare. If we exclude words containing the diphthong *oo* (*school, wool,* etc.), we are left with fewer than two dozen *ol* words, and one third of these are chemical terms:

control	*idol*	*viol*	*alcohol*	*menthol*
gambol	*carol*	*pistol*	*aerosol*	*glycol*
capitol	*patrol*	*parasol*	*vitriol*	*petrol*
extol				*ethanol*

Nor are there many words that end in *il*. If we exclude words that contain the diphthongs *oi* and *ai* (*oil, soil, ail, tail,* etc.), we are left with about three dozen words:

anvil	*pupil*	*tonsil*	*utensil*
fossil	*devil*	*council*	

Note that all the words in this group have a single *l*. When a suffix that begins with an *l* is added, it only appears that the *l* has been doubled.

diagonally	*rascally*	*vertically*

Many dictionaries offer *duffel bag* and *duffle coat* on the same page. Since there are no *fel* words in English, both words should follow the spelling rule—*duffle bag* and *duffle coat*.

CHAPTER 41

Using ize, ise, yze, yse

There are a great number of words that end in these spellings. The spelling rules that govern them are quite clear and there are few anomalies. The *ize* suffix has been in use for about four hundred years. It means *"to become like or resemble"* and is most commonly added to adjectives and nouns to create verbs. Lately, this suffix has become so popular that some experts believe that it is overused. Many writers refuse to use such words as *finalize* or *prioritize*, but these words are now common usage and are in the dictionaries. If they follow the spelling rules and their meaning is clear, they should be accepted.

In American spelling the suffix is almost always *ize*, whereas in British spelling it is often *ise*. However, this is rapidly changing, and the *ize* spelling is now all but universally accepted.

Spelling rule #1: If the ending is an unaccented final syllable, it will probably be a suffix and will be spelled *ize*:

modernize	*pasteurize*	*vocalize*	*standardize*

Spelling rule #2: If the final syllable is accented, it is probably part of the root and will be spelled *ise*—*surprise* and *revise*. There are, however, a few words in this group that do not accent the final syllable—*chastise* and *clockwise*.

Note that *yze* is mainly restricted to scientific terms. Very few commonly used words have this ending:

analyze	*paralyze*	*electrolyze*	*hydrolyze*

Curiously enough, the British spell some of these words with *yse*, thereby adding yet another ending for them to worry about, but one less for us in America. There are no commonly used words that end in *yse*.

Only about ten percent of the words in this general category are spelled with *ise*, and these can be divided into a few small groups.

(1) Words based upon the old English word *wise*, meaning either "*intelligence*" or "*direction.*" These words are usually compounds:

wise	*worldly-wise*	*contrariwise*
unwise	*clockwise*	*edgewise*
nowise	*counterclockwise*	*endwise*
otherwise	*likewise*	*lengthwise*
streetwise		*slantwise*

(2) Words ending in *vise* or *cise*, which are Latin roots and not suffixes:

advise	*revise*	*excise*
improvise	*circumcise*	*exorcise*
devise	*exercise*	*incise*

(3) A small group of words ending in *rise:*

rise	*apprise*	*enterprise*	*uprise*
arise	*comprise*	*reprise*	*emprise*
moonrise	*sunrise*	*surprise*	*prise*

(4) Four words that end in *mise:*

demise	*surmise*	*remise*	*compromise*

(5) Two words that end in *uise*—*guise* and *disguise.*

And of course there are always a few words that refuse to fit themselves into any group:

advertise	*franchise*	*merchandise*	*chastise*	*despise*

Three of these words are in the process of change. The word *advertise* is now quite often spelled *advertize*. If we are prepared to accept *advert* as a noun, then the verbs *advertize* and *advertizing* are logically correct. The words *franchise* and *merchandise* are nouns. When they are used as verbs, the spelling ought to be *franchize* and *merchandize*.

Note that some words that are spelled with *ize* do not belong in this category because the *ize* is not a true suffix or because it is part of a diphthong:

assize	*capsize*	*prize*	*seize*	*baize*

But there are two words that reverse the rule—*prize* and *prise*. Spelled with a *z* it is a noun, but spelled with an *s* it is a verb.

There are about a dozen words that are spelled with *ise* that are even more anomalous because of their various pronunciations:

paradise	*valise*	*premise*	*imprecise*
chemise	*expertise*	*cerise*	*promise*
precise	*concise*	*mortise*	*treatise*

In review, we can see that the four suffixes can be reduced to two major groups. In the first and largest, we have the words ending in *ize*. In the second, we have words that end in *ise*. These words may be nouns, verbs, or adjectives, but the *ise* ending is almost never a suffix. There are very few true anomalies. With *advertize*, *franchize*, *finalize*, and a few other words, it is interesting to note that the change in spelling is toward the spelling rule, not away from it.

CHAPTER 42

Using ical, acle, icle

*H*ere is another set of suffixes that appear at first glance to be tricky but are actually quite simple.

Spelling rule #1: Words ending in *ical* are almost always adjectives. There are well over three hundred of them. A tiny sample:

chemical	cyclical	logical	lyrical	clinical
musical	cubical	statistical	angelical	medical

Spelling rule #2: Words ending in *acle* and *icle* are almost always nouns. There are about three dozen of them.

barnacle	obstacle	article	cubicle

Note that there is very little difference between the two suffixes acle and icle. Logically, they should all be spelled with the icle ending, but, because of the origin of the root word, we have a division:

(1) Words ending in *acle:*

debacle	barnacle	binnacle	manacle	spectacle
pinnacle	tabernacle	coracle	oracle	tentacle
miracle	obstacle	pentacle	receptacle	

(2) And words ending in *icle:*

cubicle	vehicle	follicle	particle	canticle
chicle	vesicle	article	radicle	cuticle
ossicle	fascicle	pedicle	ventricle	testicle
icicle		chronicle		clavicle

Note that although the words in this group have an ending that sounds rather like *cul* there is no commonly used English word that actually ends in *cul*.

And only four words end in *col:*

glycol	caracol	protocol	col

Chapter 43

Using ant, ent, ance, ence, ense

*H*undreds of words end in *ant* or *ent*, but, alas, time and usage have created such a tangle that there are few clear rules. This group of words contains nouns, adjectives, and even some verbs. The problem can be traced all the way back to the roots of many of these words and involves certain Latin conjugations. Obviously, this is no help to the modern student, and so the best we can do is list a few basic rules and a number of guidelines. .

The most common ending is *ent*, with roughly seventy-five percent of the words in this group. But there are so many words involved that a large number end in *ant*. Generally speaking, most of the words that end in *ant* are nouns, whereas most of the words ending in *ent* are adjectives. This, again alas, is by no means a general rule.

Spelling rule #1: After a hard c or a hard g, the suffix will be *ant*:

communicant	applicant	arrogant	fumigant
lubricant	intoxicant	elegant	litigant

Spelling rule #2: After a soft c or a soft g, the suffix will be *ent*:

innocent	adolescent	urgent	pungent
reticent	magnificent	convergent	intelligent

Spelling rule #3: There must be continuity:

resistant	resistance	different	difference
significant	significance	resurgent	resurgence

Generally, the suffix *ent* indicates a quality or a characteristic. The word will probably be an adjective:

excellent	efficient	complacent	negligent
obsolescent	absent	intelligent	impotent

Generally, the suffix *ant* indicates a person or thing that does something. The word will probably be a noun:

pretendant	fumigant	lubricant
confidant	deodorant	occupant
contestant	assistant	defendant

A great number of words that end in *ent* or *ant* do not fit into either category, however, because the ending does not form a suffix:

cement	relent	plant
present	current	rampant
innocent	currant	infant

Just to add to the confusion, we have a group of words that end in *ense*:

dense	condense	offense	immense
defense	license	nonsense	incense
intense	tense	expense	recompense
sense	dispense	pretense	suspense

What is fascinating about this group of *ense* words is that the British spell some of them just the opposite way:

pretense	pretence	defense	defence
offense	offence	license	licence

On the eastern side of the Atlantic, *licence* is the noun while the verb is *license*. On the western side of the Atlantic, *license* is used as both noun and verb.

There are times when the different ending gives the word a completely different meaning:

dependent	dependant	current	currant
confident	confidant	valence	valance

CHAPTER 44

Using sy and cy

$\mathcal{H}$undreds of English words end in either *sy* or *cy*. Words ending in *cy* are most common and outnumber the *sy* words by about four to one.

One of the differences between these two endings is the sound. The *cy* has a hard *s* sound while the *sy* is soft. Compare *fancy* and *daisy*.

Spelling rule #1: The suffix cy is used to form nouns from root words that end in t, te, nt, and tic:

urgent	urgency	truant	truancy
frequent	frequency	democrat	democracy
lunatic	lunacy	accurate	accuracy
pregnant	pregnancy	idiot	idiocy
private	privacy		

Spelling rule #2: The cy ending may also denote rank, office, or title:

regency	confederacy	excellency
presidency	papacy	episcopacy

Spelling rule #3: No commonly used verbs end in cy. These words will be mostly nouns, but there are a few adjectives which come from roots that end in c or ce:

icy	racy	juicy	saucy
spicy	bouncy	lacy	fleecy

Spelling rule #4: The sy ending is also used to create nouns or adjectives. The adjectives in this group tend to be informal or diminutive:

dressy	cutesy	cosy	folksy	tipsy
nosy	bossy	choosy	lousy	teensy

A number of words that end in *sy* are medical terms that end in *epsy*, *opsy*, etc.:

autopsy	leprosy	epilepsy
biopsy	catalepsy	narcolepsy

But no commonly used verbs end in *sy*.

Needless to say, there are numerous words, both nouns and adjectives, that end in *sy* or *cy* where these endings are not suffixes:

mercy	*fancy*	*busy*	*daisy*
policy	*discrepancy*	*clumsy*	*queasy*

CHAPTER 45

Using igh, ough, augh

$\mathcal{W}$ithout a doubt. the most annoying spellings in the English language are the ancient *igh*, *ough*, and *augh*. They are thousand-year-old relics that should have vanished centuries ago, but never did. The *gh* sound was once pronounced and can still be heard in the Scottish pronunciation of *loch*, but though the spelling remains, the sound has disappeared from general speech.

A great many popular words contain one of these spellings and there are no rules to help the student. The best we can do is list the most commonly used words according to their various sounds.

Note that the British pronounce *slough* to rhyme with *cow*. In North America, the word *slough* has become two words. When referring to a swamp or mud hole, it is *slue*. When it is used as a verb to describe the removal of a reptile's skin, or a similar action, it is *sluff*.

(1) The long *i* sound with *igh*:

height	wright	right	tight	delight
sleight	bight	alright	blight	plight
slight	light	knight	night	flight
fright	alight		sight	fight
	might		bright	

Note that *height* and *sleight* are the only commonly used words that use the *ei* spelling.

(2) The f sound with augh and ough:

laugh	tough	rough	cough
draught	trough	enough	slough

Note that *laugh* and *draught* are the only commonly used words that use the *au* spelling, and *draught* has now been largely replaced by *draft*.

(3) The long *u* sound with *ough—through* and *slough*.

(4) The *ow* sound with *ough*:

sough	bough	doughty
plough		drought

(5) The *oh* sound with *ough*:

though	furlough	borough
although	thorough	dough

(6) The *aw* sound with *ough*:

ought	thought	nought
fought	brought	wrought
sought	bought	besought

(7) The *aw* sound with *augh*:

aught	caught	taught	daughter
naught	onslaught	haughty	distraught
naughty	fraught	slaughter	

Note *nought* or *naught*. The *nought* spelling is preferable.
Note also that *aught* and *ought* have different meanings.

(8) The *ay* sound with *eigh* and *aigh*:

eight	inveigh	neigh	freight	weight
aweigh	weigh	neighbor	sleigh	straight

Note that *straight* is the only word in this group that uses the *ai* spelling.

There are additional words that contain the gh spelling:

ghost	spaghetti	yoghurt
ghastly	shillelagh	dinghy
aghast	moghul	carragheen

Note that the Indian word *dingi* later gained an unnecessary *h*. The words *ghost*, *ghastly*, and *aghast* were originally spelled *goost*, *gastly*, and *agast*.

Fortunately, some changes are slowly beginning to appear. The *h* has been dropped from three of the nine words listed above:

carrageen	yogurt	mogul

89

In the *igh* group, the spellings *brite*, *flite*, *lite*, and *nite* are now widely used in advertizing and in trade names. In time, this spelling will be in general use.

NOTES:

(1) In the *ough* group, the new spellings *tho*, *altho*, and *thoro* are now minimally acceptable and often used.

(2) *Boro* in place of *borough* is quite common in placenames.

(3) *Doughnut* is almost always spelled *donut*.

(4) *Beseeched* is now more commonly used than *besought*.

(5) The spelling *thru* is quite popular. It is widely used on road signs and in the transportation industry and on restaurants that offer a "*drive-thru.*" Although it has been around for over one hundred years, it has not yet been fully accepted.

(6) The word *plough* has been replaced by *plow*.

(7) The awkward word *drought* is pronounced in a number of interesting ways. The most common are *drout* and *drouth*.

(8) In the *f* group, the board game of draughts is called checkers in North America and the word *draught* is now spelled *draft*.

CHAPTER 46

Using f, ff, ph, gh

*T*he *f* sound can be produced in four different ways, but by far the most common is the single *f*, which can be found at the beginning, in the middle, or at the end of a word. Only about sixty words end in a single *f*. Many of the nouns among them will change the *f* to *ve* when made into a plural.

Spelling rule #1: A single *f* is used at the beginning of a word:

father	*fly*	*funny*
former	*farther*	*fruit*

Spelling rule #2: A single *f* is used when it follows a long vowel sound:

waif	*chief*	*sofa*
leaf	*wife*	*hoof*

Spelling rule #3: A single *f* is used when it is preceded by a consonant:

dwarf	*surf*	*golf*
shelf	*half*	*scarf*

Spelling rule #4: The double *f* is used after a short vowel sound. These words are usually single syllable words. In multi-syllable words, the double *f* is always preceded by a short vowel sound.

gaff	*cliff*	*traffic*	*different*
sniff	*scoff*	*coffee*	*offering*
stuff	*staff*	*muffler*	*effigy*

Note that no commonly used English word starts with a double *f*.

A single *f* may occasionally follow a short vowel sound when the *f* is followed by a consonant. These words will usually be compounds or the *f* will be followed by the letter *t*.

antifreeze	*fifteen*	*lift*	*croft*
cauliflower	*fifty*	*raft*	*soft*

Anomalies include *of, if, chef, clef,* and *pilaf.*

There are two other ways to produce the *f* sound. We can use *gh* or *ph.* The *gh* digraph is the least common of the *f* sounds, but, unfortunately, it is attached to some very popular words:

cough	*trough*	*enough*	*draught*
rough	*tough*	*laugh*	*slough*

Most of these very old words did not originally have this *gh* ending. All but one were spelled with a simple *h* and were pronounced rather like the Scottish *loch* or the Irish *lough.*

cough	*coghen*	*enough*	*genoh*
rough	*ruh*	*trough*	*troh*
draught	*draht*	*laugh*	*hlah*
tough	*toh*	*slough*	*sluh*

While the British still cling to draught and draughty, in North America we have long ago switched to draft and drafty. Similarly, while they spell it slough and pronounce it to rhyme with cow, we are in the process of switching to slue and sluff, depending on how the word is used.

As for the other words, their days are numbered. At the present time no dictionary contains the words *tuff, coff,* or *laff.* but they have already made their debut in comic strips, colloquial writing, advertising, and other light or humorous pieces. It is inevitable that these more logical and phonetically correct spellings will eventually replace the archaic, anachronistic forms.

Making the *f* sound with *ph* is quite another matter. Almost all of the sixty or more commonly used words, from *photo* and *phone* to *phobia* and *graph,* plus countless scientific terms, are of Greek origin and are now deeply imbedded in our language.

phantom	*phonetic*	*phosphorus*	*photograph*
pharmacy	*phoenix*	*nymph*	*telephone*
	phenomenon	*triumph*	

We must wonder why the ancient translators chose to use *ph* when the Greeks used a single letter *phi* (Φ) or why they did not simply use the *f.* Many languages, most notably Spanish, logically use the *f*:

fotografia	*farmacia*	*telefono*	*filosofico*

Perhaps the change is already happening. Today, the name *Stephen* is more commonly spelled *Steven,* and we also have the unaccepted but very popular *foto* for *photograph.*

Chapter 47

Using wh *and* h

*H*undreds of English words use the *wh* digraph. It usually appears at the beginning of a word and never at the end. If it occurs in the middle of a word, it will most probably be part of a compound.

Spelling rule #1: When the *wh* is followed by *a, e, i,* or *y,* the *w* is pronounced and the *h* is almost silent:

whack	*wheel*	*wheat*	*whiz*
what	*when*	*while*	*white*
whale	*where*	*whisper*	*why*

Spelling rule #2: When the *wh* is followed by *o,* some of the words have the emphasis on the *w,* but most will emphasize the *h.*

who	*whom*	*whose*	*whoop*
whole	*wholesale*	*wholly*	*whopper*
wholesome	*whore*	*whosoever*	*whoosh*

To say that the *h* is silent in the majority of these words is not quite correct. A large number of English speakers pronounce these words with a soft, almost inaudible *h* sound before the *w.* This is neither an affectation nor a mispronunciation. It simply reflects the history of almost all of these words and proves that change can sometimes take centuries.

Our Saxon forebears spelled almost all of these words with the *h* before the *w* and pronounced them that way.

hwa	*who*	*hwy*	*why*	*hweat*	*what*
hwit	*white*	*hweol*	*wheel*	*hwenne*	*when*
hal	*whole*	*hwaer*	*where*		

With the upheaval of the Norman invasion, the first two letters were reversed and the harsh initial *h* was softened as the emphasis was gradually put on the *w.* A thousand years later, however, many of us still pronounce these words in the old way.

Words in which the initial *h* is clearly pronounced are variations of *whole,* which did not have a *w,* or they are variations of *who,* which did not change. In some parts of

.... the board game of draughts is called checkers in North America and the word draught is now spelled draft.

Scotland, who is still *wha*. Today, no commonly used English word begins with *hw*.

Note that the *h* is a very useful letter. Countless words begin with *h*, and it can also be found in the middle of numerous words. As the final letter in a word, however, it is quite rare. If we exclude proper nouns such as *Allah, Utah, Isaiah,* and *Bar Mitzvah,* we are left with a small handful of commonly used words.

loofah	*rajah*	*hallelujah*	*hurrah*
purdah	*savannah*	*pariah*	*hookah*
chutzpah	*cheetah*	*messiah*	*ankh*

But half of these words have already lost the final *h* and are now often spelled as follows.

loofa	*savanna*	*raja*
chutzpa	*hooka*	*purda*

Note that a wide selection of interjections end in the letter *h*:

yeah!	*ah!*	*blah!*	*aaah!*
oh! or oh?	*bah!*	*pooh!*	*huh?*

The *h* is often called a silent letter. This is partly true. When it is sounded, it is very rarely heavily aspirated. It is silent in most of the digraphs:

chow	*dhow*	*bough*
ankh	*graph*	*rhapsody*
ash	*why*	*the*

Note that the *h* is never doubled unless it forms part of a compound word:

fishhook	*highhanded*	*beachhead*
bathhouse	*withhold*	*hitchhiker*

CHAPTER 48

Using of *and* off

$\mathcal{T}$hese two words are not true homophones. The preposition *of* has a soft *v* sound, whereas the adverb *off* has a distinct *f* sound. This puts *of* in the unique position of being the only commonly used English word in which the letter *f* has the *v* sound.

The simple preposition *of* indicates some type of relationship—distance, direction, origin, material, or identity.

*The number **of** miles*	*A dress **of** silk*
*The grass **of** the fields*	*One **of** the idle rich*

The adverb *off* is a much more interesting word. Not only can it be used by itself, but it can also form compounds or be used as a prefix or a suffix. It indicates movement away from, something unsupported, or separation.

off-price	*offshore*	*playoff*	*off-the-record*
offset	*cook-off*	*runoff*	*off-the-cuff*

Spelling rule #1: *Off* and *of* should never be used together.

Wrong:	*He stepped **off of** the bus.*
Correct:	*He stepped **off** the bus.*

Spelling rule #2. *Of* should never be used in place of *have*.

Wrong:	*I could **of** gone.*
Correct:	*I could **have** gone.*

CHAPTER 49

Using et *and* ette

*T*he French influence on the English language is still very strong. It shows itself not only in the roots of many of our words but also in present-day pronunciation and spelling. French spellings often lead to problems.

With the suffixes *et* and *ette*, the problem is when do we pronounce the *t* and when do we pronounce *et* as *ay*? We must wonder what the rules are when we pronounce the *t* in *billet* and *ballot* but not in *ballet*. Similarly, we pronounce the *t* in *banquet* but not in *bouquet*.

Traditionally, the *et* ending is pronounced *ay* as in *ballet, croquet,* and *crochet,* and the *ette* ending is pronounced *et,* as in *cassette* and *gazette.* There are over three hundred English words that end in *et* and all, except about twenty, are pronounced *et.* Many of these words are of French origin.

amulet	*basinet*	*varlet*	*fillet*	*carpet*
dulcet	*bassinet*	*bayonet*	*billet*	*lancet*
parapet	*epaulet*	*facet*	*garret*	*violet*
valet	*pellet*	*ratchet*	*scarlet*	

The following are some of the words that retain the *ay* sound.

ballet	*chalet*	*soubriquet*	*cabaret*
cachet	*sachet*	*bouquet*	*gourmet*
ricochet	*bidet*	*croquet*	*parquet*
beret	*crochet*	*buffet*	*cabriolet*

As for the *ette* ending, there are fewer than two dozen commonly used English words that are still spelled that way. A number of these are in the process of changing to the simple *et* ending.

quartette	*quartet*	*toilette*	*toilet*
quintette	*quintet*	*kitchenette*	*kitchenet*
septette	*septet*	*briquette*	*briquet*
octette	*octet*	*cigarette*	*cigaret*
palette	*pallet*	*epaulette*	*epaulet*
omelette	*omelet*	*bassinet*	

Clearly, the English language has enthusiastically adopted the diminutive suffix *ette*, but just as clearly the shorter *et* is preferred over the cumbersome *ette*, no matter how it was used in the original French. Following the healthy tradition of *adopt* and *adapt*, it has now been anglicized.

There are times when the French spelling and/or pronunciation must be retained in order to differentiate between homophones. When the *t* is pronounced in *fillet*, it has a number of meanings in woodwork, dressmaking, and metal work. When the ending is pronounced *ay*, it usually refers to meat or fish, but even this difference is slowly disappearing. The word *pallet* likewise has numerous meanings ranging from a straw bed to a wooden support for freight. The paint board used by an artist, however, is spelled *palette*. The words *kitchenette* and *dinette* are purely 20th-century American inventions.

Chapter 50

Using less *and* ness

Off and *of* should never be used together.

The suffixes *less* and *ness* are extremely popular and deserve some attention because the spelling rules that apply to them are remarkably similar.

Less is primarily a comparative and is most commonly used as an adjective suffix indicating a lack of something. *Ness*, on the other hand, is a suffix used to form abstract nouns.

Spelling rule #1: The suffix *less* is added to a word without any changes. If the root has a silent *e* it will be retained. If the root ends in *l*, the silent *e* is retained. Change the *y* to *i*.

worthless	*senseless*	*soulless*
childless	*useless*	*merciless*
endless	*skilless*	*penniless*
tireless	*tailless*	*pitiless*

Spelling rule #2: The suffix *ness* is added to a word without any changes. If the root has a silent *e*, it is retained. If the root ends in an *n*, it is retained. Change the *y* to *i*.

darkness	*sameness*	*openness*
kindness	*politeness*	*kindliness*
goodness	*thinness*	*heartiness*
blueness	*suddenness*	*heaviness*

Unlike *full*, these two suffixes do not drop the extra consonant. The double *s* is retained, even when both suffixes are used with the same root word.

soullessness	*heartlessness*	*worthlessness*

When used as a separate word before a noun, *less* modifies only singular nouns of quantity. Plural nouns must use the word *fewer*.

Paul has **less** money than Peter.	Paul has **fewer** dollars than Peter.
I take **less** sugar in my tea.	I take **fewer** sugar lumps in my tea.
There is **less** traffic.	There are **fewer** cars.

CHAPTER 51

Using fore *and* for

The prefixes *fore* and *for* should not be confused with the preposition *for* nor with the number *four*. Also, not all the words that begin with *for* or *fore* have prefixes.

Fore means "*before or in front of.*" There are a number of words that contain this prefix:

forecast   forerunner   forecourt   forefront   foreword

The prefix *for* often has a negative meaning of opposition or rejection. There are only about a dozen words in this group.

forbid   forfend   forget   forfeit   forlorn

With the *e* and without *it*, we have two words with quite different meanings.

forebear   forbear   foregoing   forgo

Note that a number of other words begin with for or fore but the syllable is not a prefix:

forest   fortunate   ford   force   formation   forensic

CHAPTER 52

Using anti, ante, anto

These prefixes can be confusing, but they are good examples of how one small letter can make a remarkable difference in the meaning of a word.

The Latin prefix *ante* means "before or in front of":

antecedent	antebellum	antediluvian	antechamber

The Greek prefix *anti* means "against or opposed to." There are hundreds of words that use this prefix and new ones are created every day.

anticoagulant	antitank	antisocial
anticlockwise	antiseptic	anticyclone

But there is only one commonly used word that begins with *anto*—antonym, a word opposite in meaning to another word.

There are numerous other words that begin with *ante* or *anti* but do not contain either of these prefixes:

antelope	antenna	antique	antics

Probably the most commonly used example of *ante* is the A.M. abbreviation we use to indicate the time before noon. It means *ante meridian*. This is the only time that the prefix is separated from the rest of the word.

CHAPTER 53

Using *in, into, on, onto*

*I*n, *into, on,* and *onto* are often used incorrectly, not only in casual conversation, but also in formal discussion and in the pages of newspapers and periodicals whose editors should know better.

Some writers seem to think that *in* and *into* are interchangeable or have the same meaning. They are wrong. *In* states a place. *The man was **in** the car. Into* states a direction or movement. *The man got **into** the car.* Likewise, the common expression *Go jump **in** the lake* ought to be *Go jump **into** the lake,* but it's too late to change it now. Those of us who care about clear communication should always insist that *The lady walked **in** the room* means that she was already in the room when she decided to walk. *The lady walked **into** the room* means that she was outside and she entered the room.

Similarly, *on* means a location or position. *The stamp was **on** the letter,* but *She stuck the stamp **onto** the letter* means that she attached the stamp to the letter.

The word *onto* seems to be gradually vanishing. It appears less and less in conversation or in print and its place is being taken by the simple *on* which now serves double duty as position and action. *"The passengers got **on** the plane,"* and *"The passengers were **on** the plane,"* are both quite common now. This is unfortunate because if clarity in communication is our primary aim, then the misuse of one word that aids clear communication is to be regretted.

CHAPTER 54

The Schwa

Probably the most commonly used example of ante is the A.M. abbreviation we use to indicate the time before noon. It means ante meridian. This is the only time that the prefix is separated from the rest of the word.

The schwa, which is given as the symbol ə in the International Phonetic Alphabet (IPA), was introduced into English barely one hundred years ago. It comes from a Hebrew word meaning "no vowel," and was first used to indicate those instances where the vowel was not clearly defined but sounded vaguely like *uh*.

Somewhere in the middle of the 20th century, the humble schwa became immensely popular, and people who ought to have known better began to sprinkle it everywhere. Lazy lexicographers and careless editors stuck in a schwa wherever they thought it would fit. Needless to say, spelling, diction, and correct pronunciation suffered and have continued to suffer.

Because it has been so greatly overused, everybody should look upon the schwa with deep suspicion. There are countless examples in dictionaries and text books where the author has used a schwa when anybody who cared to pronounce the word correctly would see that it was not necessary. This infatuation with the schwa is merely a form of phonic laziness.

It cannot be denied that the schwa has its place. The endings *tion* and *sion* are usually schwas, as are most of the *le* endings and many of the *er* endings, but there are enough legitimate schwa sounds without phonic laziness producing more. Since poor pronunciation leads inevitably to poor spelling, both the teacher and the student should sound a word out carefully before deciding whether or not it contains a schwa.

CHAPTER 55

Silent Consonants:
h, g, k, p, w, b, l, n, t, c, d, s, m, r, ch

*M*ost languages have one or two letters that may occasionally be silent, depending on the spelling or the punctuation. Thanks to its history of borrowing, however, English clearly has more than its fair share of letters that are sometimes not pronounced. In fact, almost all of the letters of the alphabet are, at one time or another, silent letters.

There are two main reasons why we have so many silent letters. First, the letter is part of the original word which has changed over time with, perhaps, the addition of affixes or compounding. The resulting words have left us with letters that we no longer pronounce. Second, imported words that have not yet been fully assimilated and anglicized sometimes contain silent letters. There are many examples of borrowed words that have been in our dictionaries for generations and probably never will be anglicized.

Because vowels are often silent, especially when they are part of a diphthong, we shall look only at the silent consonants. For the silent *e*, see Chapter 6.

The most common of the silent letters is the *h*, which can appear at the beginning of a word, in the middle, or at the end. It appears in an extraordinary variety of words and is usually followed by a vowel.

honor	*rhythm*	*wharf*	*pyrrhic*
honest	*rhubarb*	*dinghy*	*exhibit*
heir	*ghost*	*exhaust*	*catarrh*
rheumatic	*thyme*	*diarrhea*	*myrrh*

Almost as common is the silent *g*, which appears most frequently as the initial letter of a word but can also be found in the middle of a word. The silent *g* is almost always followed by an *m* or an *n*:

diaphragm	*gnaw*	*campaign*	*design*
phlegm	*gnarled*	*sign*	*impugn*
gnat	*foreign*	*reign*	*poignant*

The silent *k* usually appears at the beginning of a word and is almost always followed by *n*:

knack	knit	know
knot	knee	knuckle

The silent *p* is quite versatile. It can appear at the end, in the middle, or at the beginning of a word. The majority (but not all) of these words are of Greek origin:

psalm	ptomaine	psychosis	receipt	raspberry
pneumatic	pneumonia	ptarmigan	cupboard	coup

The silent *w* most often appears at the beginning of a word and is usually followed by *r*, though there are exceptions:

write	wry	awry	two
wretch	wrong	playwright	answer
wriggle	wrap	sword	

The silent *b* is usually found at the end or near the end of a word. In most cases. it follows the letter *m*:

lamb	limb	tomb	debt	subtle
plumb	climb	comb	doubt	

The silent *l* usually appears in the middle of a word and is followed by a consonant. It is most often preceded by the letter *a*:

salmon	chalk	talk	psalm	should	could
half	alms	calf	folk	yolk	

The silent *n* is almost always found at the end of a word and usually follows the letter *m*:

autumn	solemn	column	damn	condemn	hymn

If we exclude all the words that use *tch*, we can see that the silent *t* is usually preceded by the letter *s*:

listen	castle	fasten	whistle	often	mortgage
wrestle	thistle	rustle	christen	soften	

The silent *c* usually follows the letter *s*, but there are some exceptions:

scent	ascend	crescent	muscle
fluorescent	obsolescent	reminiscent	indict
science	conscience	scissors	czar

Whether or not the *d* is silent depends on how we pronounce a word. Most of us like to believe that we pronounce the silent *d*, but most of us do not. It usually appears before a *j* or a *g*.

adjudicate	adjust	budget
adjacent	dredger	handsome

There is a tiny group of words that contain a silent *s*:

isle	lisle	chamois
island	viscount	corps (both the p and
aisle	chassis	the s are silent)

The silent *m* is quite rare—see *mnemonic*.

The silent *r* is a special case. When it follows a vowel, it is sometimes pronounced and sometimes either not pronounced or voiced so softly that it is almost silent. It depends upon one's regional accent.

argue	ford	first	firm
other	ordinary	burned	heart
turn	butcher	farmer	murder

The *ch* can produce a number of sounds. It can have its own *ch* sound, the *sh* sound, or the *k* sound. There is one word in which the *ch* is silent—*yacht*. Note that words that contain the silent *gh* are covered in earlier chapters.

CHAPTER 56

Hyphens

*T*he hyphen is very useful when properly used. Unfortunately, it was heavily overused in the past and this has caused a reaction with some experts, who suggest that it be abandoned. It makes very little sense to throw out the baby with the bathwater *(bath-water? bath water?)* because the rules are quite clear.

The purpose of the hyphen is to join two words, such as light and house, to form a single word. At first, the hyphen was used and we had *light-house,* but after a few years the hyphen disappeared and we now have the compound word *lighthouse.* Not every noun and adjective combination should be made into a compound word or hyphenated. A red car is just a red car, but a *sportscar* is a special type of car and deserves to be a compound like *sportsman.* The spelling rule is quite logical.

Spelling rule: The hyphen should only be used when its absence might cause confusion.

There might be confusion if a compound were to be joined at two identical vowels. Is it or is it not a diphthong?

re-echo	*re-enter*	*co-operation*	*co-educational*
anti-aircraft	*de-escalate*	*re-educate*	*co-operate*
semi-invalid	*blue-eyed*	*de-ice*	

When writing numbers in words, we hyphenate fractions and all numbers from twenty-one to ninety-nine:

two-thirds	*three-sixteenths*	*twenty-one*	*ninety-nine*

Combinations of more than two words should be hyphenated:

mother-in-law	*down-to-earth*	*courts-martial*
ladies-in-waiting	*know-it-all*	

Somewhere in the middle of the 20th century, the humble schwa became immensely popular, and people who ought to have known better began to sprinkle it everywhere. Lazy lexicographers and careless editors stuck in a schwa wherever they thought it would fit. Needless to say, spelling, diction, and correct pronunciation suffered and have continued to suffer.

We hyphenate a prefix that is used with a word that must have a capital letter or any other combination of proper nouns:

neo-Nazi	*anti-American*	*pre-Victorian*
Anglo-French	*Italian-American*	

When there may be confusion between words that are spelled alike except for the hyphen, the hyphen can make a difference in meaning:

re-cover recover	*re-sign resign*	*re-creation recreation*

The hyphen may occasionally be used for emphasis:

ex-wife	*ex-convict*	*ex-member*

Note that word blends are new words created by putting together parts of other words without using hyphens,

motel = motor + hotel
brunch = late breakfast + early lunch = brunch
guesstimate = a good scientific guess

CHAPTER 57

Names

Generally speaking, names do not follow spelling rules and we should not expect them to do so. Many names have been modernized and anglicized over the years, but there are just as many that retain their ancient spellings. Such names can be both an inconvenience and a matter of great personal pride to their owners.

The names of foreign countries and cities do not always translate well, especially if they must be adapted from a different alphabet. When we browse through old atlases, we can see that the spellings of many cities and countries have changed a number of times over the years.

OLDER	NEWER	OLDER	NEWER
Peking	*Beijing*	*Koweit*	*Kuwait*
Canton	*Guangdong*	*Koran*	*Quran*
Kamerun	*Cameroon*	*Akabah*	*Aquaba*
Mecca	*Makkah*		

There are difficulties involved when we do try to make a foreign name fit English spelling. Sometimes the name is anglicized, and *Italia* becomes *Italy*, or *España* becomes *Spain*, but usually we attempt to produce something that is close to the original, no matter what the spelling. If we applied strict spelling rules to *Iraq*, for example, it would have to be *Irack* because in English the *q* may not stand alone and a *k* does not usually follow a short vowel. But *Iraq* it is.

Over the centuries, a whole host of names, both English and foreign, have become part of our everyday language. Thanks to Louis Pasteur, our milk is *pasteurized*. Thanks to Captain Charles Boycott, we *boycott* what we don't like. Thanks to a Cervantes hero, we consider some things *quixotic*. Thanks to a titled Englishman who wouldn't stop playing cards to eat his dinner, we eat *sandwiches*. There are quite a few fascinating books on this subject. Most of these name-words lose their capital letters as they cease to be proper nouns. The element *einsteinium*, for example, has lost it, even though the word *Fahrenheit* still retains the capital *f*.

Whether the spelling changes or not, whether the pronunciation changes or not, another useful word has been acquired and yet another exotic jewel has been added to that treasury of words that we call English.

CHAPTER 58

Linguistic Terminology

*W*hen we study English spelling, it is inevitable that we will encounter one or more technical terms. While the spelling is no great problem, the meanings of the terms are often confusing.

A *homograph* is a word that is spelled the same as another word but has a different meaning, which is usually evident in context. It may or may not have the same sound:

| bear | bear | lead | lead | row | row |

A *homophone* is a word that is pronounced the same as another word but has a different meaning. It may or may not be spelled the same way.

| heir | air | night | knight | pair | pear |

A *homonym* is a word that is both a *homophone* and a *homograph* because it is the same as another in both sound and spelling but has a different meaning.

| bear | bear | spruce | spruce | chase | chase |

Antonyms are words that are opposite from each other in meaning:

| ugly | beautiful | dark | light | fat | thin | short | tall |

Synonyms are words with the same, or almost the same meaning as other words. We commonly find synonyms in the thesaurus:

| heavy | weighty | big | large | boring | uninteresting |

Heteronyms are words spelled the same as other words but have a different sound and meaning:

read	read	lead	lead	address	address
sow	sow	invalid	invalid	live	live
contract	contract	wind	wind	refuse	refuse

A *diphthong* is two vowels that together create a single sound:

aa	kraal	eu	aneurism	oo	look
ae	Aeolian	ey	prey	ou	shout
ai	pail	ie	field	oy	coyly
au	nautical	ii	Hawaii	ua	persuade
ay	play	io	action	ue	true
ea	peace	oa	boat	uo	fluoride
ee	feed	ao	pharaoh	uu	vacuum
ei	weigh	oe	shoe	uy	buy
eo	eons	oi	soil		

The *digraph* is two consonants that together create a unique sound:

ch	sh	ph	gh	th

Note that there is a great deal of confusion, even among the experts, over the exact meaning of many of these terms. Some see *digraph* and *diphthong* as the same thing. Some use *homonym* to cover both *homographs* and *homophones.* Others just lump all the terms together and call them *phonemes* and *graphemes,* words that sound alike and words that are written alike.

CHAPTER 59
Acronyms

*O*ne of the many marvels of the English language is the way in which it borrows words from any and every source and, if a word is not readily available, we manufacture a new one by compounding or contraction. Or we just make up a new word.

Acronyms are a special group of manufactured words that go through a process of assimilation that is often quite rapid, though sometimes they are never fully assimilated. The radar set did not even exist before 1940, yet today *radar* is almost a household word. The word is made up from the initial letters of *Radio Detection And Receiving*. During World War II, servicemen quickly called it RADAR, and it even more speedily lost its uppercase spelling and became *radar*. Ten years later, the *Self-Contained Underwater Breathing Apparatus* was invented, and, almost overnight, we had the highly popular *scuba* outfit. These are just two of the better known acronyms. The advent of the personal computer has produced a steady stream of new and exotic words, many of which started life as acronyms and rapidly became regular words.

The creation and assimilation of acronyms has created its own set of spelling rules.

Spelling rule: Brand new acronyms consist of capital letters with periods between each letter. Intermediate stage acronyms are still in capital letters, but they have lost the periods. Mature acronyms have split into two groups:
(1) Names or proper nouns, spelled in capital letters with no periods:

UNESCO	*NATO*	*NASA*

(2) Regular words with neither capitals nor periods:

radar	*laser*	*posh*
flak	*scuba*	*ram and rom*
sonar	*jeep*	

Note that not all abbreviations become acronyms. For example, the UN, MI5, the FBI, and IRA are always pronounced as separate letters.

CHAPTER 60

Dictionaries

$\mathcal{A}$ good dictionary is indispensable. English spelling is so complex that nobody can claim that they have a perfect grasp and that they do not need a dictionary. But there is a huge variety of dictionaries. They come in all sizes and cover all subjects. There are scientific dictionaries and medical dictionaries, and there are dictionaries of almost every known language. There are dictionaries of proverbs, of quotes, of slang, of strange words, and of obsolete words. One might wonder if there is a dictionary for every subject under the sun.

Many publishers, both small and large, have produced a dictionary and many of them call their product a "Webster's dictionary." Because the name is not a protected name, as the name Merriam-Webster is, there is nothing to prevent any publisher from using it, and many do. Since no modern dictionary is even remotely similar to Noah Webster's original masterpiece, the name has no real meaning today.

The accuracy of a dictionary can not be taken for granted. A detailed study of any three or four dictionaries would very quickly produce scores of disagreements and even some contradictions regarding the correct spelling of some words. Unfortunately, when there is a difference in spelling, most dictionaries play it safe and offer the reader a choice of what is available with little, if any, explanation.

Modern publishers do not tread the path first blazed by Noah Webster. For the most part, they are merely compilers of word lists, content to stick to the status quo. They see themselves as recorders of what exists today with no duty to give more than the necessary facts and, perhaps, the etymology of the word. They sell their product by trumpeting the number of words they have listed and increase the size of the book by adding material that better belongs in an atlas or encyclopedia.

Few, if any, dictionaries attempt to influence spelling by coming down firmly in favor of a particular spelling that logically follows the spelling rules as against a spelling that is an aberration. Also, most dictionaries are hesitant, almost reluctant, to accept new spellings despite the fact that English spelling is constantly changing.

Noah Webster would be most annoyed. He saw his dictionary as a teaching tool to be used as a powerful influence on the language. He believed that a dictionary should lead, not follow, and that it should do so energetically. He forced Americans, and the world, to re-evaluate English spelling in order to make it more logical. If Webster had been content to simply list all the words as they then existed—complete with illogical spellings—the American version of the English language would not be what it is today and Webster would have vanished into obscurity like the dictionary compilers who preceded him.

CHAPTER 61

Accent—American or British?

*R*eaders who are learning English may wonder if they should try to acquire an American accent or a British accent. The answer is quite simple. Neither.

Today in England alone, there are over twenty regional accents that most Englishmen recognize and many more local accents that are not so easy to define. Educated, middle-class Englishmen attempt to speak standard, or BBC, English, but there is also the problem of class, a very important element in English life. Members of the upper class define themselves by speaking in an exaggerated manner, while the lower classes continue to use the regional accents. The end result is that the national language is badly fragmented and no single region may be said to speak in a "typically English" accent.

The pattern is similar in North America, where there are numerous regional accents that everybody recognizes and many less easily definable accents. Fortunately, North Americans do not have an upper-class accent to complicate matters. Most educated, upper- and middle-class North Americans speak what is called "middle American," while the lower classes tend to emphasize their regional accents. But there is no "typically American" accent.

The English have a saying, "If you hear somebody speaking perfectly correct English, they're probably not English." Obviously, the student will not attempt to copy any of the regional accents, but one pitfall that should be avoided is the affectation among the middle and upper class of turning many of the *a* sounds into *ah* sounds.

The spelling rule is clear. "Unless it is modified by a silent *e* or other modifying vowels, the *a* is almost always a short vowel, especially if it is followed by a doubled consonant. The *a* only sounds like *ah* when followed by the letter *r*." For example: *bar, car, far, jar, star,* etc. These have the *ah* sound, but *class, pass, ass, grass, glass,* etc. do not.

This affectation is quite popular, and the student will hear a great number of words that have a short *a* pronounced as if the *a* were a long vowel. For example: *passport, banana, can't, example, plant, fast, glance, dance, chance.* It becomes ludicrous when even the names of foreign countries are mispronounced and *Iran, Pakistan,* and *Afghanistan* become *Irahn, Pahkistahn,* and *Ahfgahnistahn.*

The English-speaking population of North America is well over 300 million, while the combined population of all the other English-speaking nations—Australia, New Zealand, the United Kingdom, South Africa, the West Indies—is less then 100 million. North America is also the greatest exporter of movies and TV shows and has the largest number of foreign students studying in its universities, so it is obvious that the North American version of the English language is the dominant version. There are two major pitfalls that the foreign student must avoid.

First, many North Americans have great difficulty pronouncing an internal *t.* Almost daily you will hear *innernet (internet), innernational (international), innerested (interested), budder (butter), bedder (better), badder (batter), liddle (little), waiding (waiting), seddle (settle), gedding (getting), ledder (letter),* and many other poorly pronounced words. The student should carefully pronounce the internal *t* whenever it is supposed to be pronounced.

Second, in a great many parts of North America the sound of the vowel *o* is changed to a. *Hot* becomes *hat, got* becomes *gat,* and *Colorado* becomes *Calarado.* This is often, but not always, a regional accent, and North Americans from New York to Toronto to Los Angeles can be heard mispronouncing the letter *o* in this way. The student should always take care to pronounce this vowel correctly, bearing in mind that if we hope for clear communication, enunciation is as important as pronunciation.

End

About the Author

*J*OHN FULFORD's first experience as a teacher was in a lonely, one-room school in northern Canada. Among his students that winter were some French-speaking children and half a dozen Native Americans. He survived the winter, and during his subsequent forty years of teaching he taught every grade from kindergarten to college prep. as well as adult education. He has also taught overseas.

Born in Spain of British parents, the author was educated in England and after a stint in the RAF, he worked as the advertising manager and proofreader on a small magazine in London before emigrating to Canada, where he earned his B. Ed. at the University of British Columbia in Vancouver. After moving to California, he earned his M.A. at California State University in Long Beach.

Mr Fulford was an avid book worm by the second grade and acquired his love for the English language from his mother, who was an English teacher, and from his father, who was a Fleet Street journalist and editor and a war correspondent during World War II.

His deep interest in spelling began when he was teaching English in Barcelona, Spain, where he found that many students who spoke and read English quite well, disliked writing in English because they had serious trouble with English spelling. They were, in fact, adamant that there is no logic to English spelling. Fulford argued otherwise and when he returned to North America, he delved deeper into the history of the English language and gradually worked out the many rules that govern English spelling.

This book is the result of twenty years of serious research into English spelling, including a study of the writings of Noah Webster, post-graduate courses in linguistics and a unique computer program. It also gave the author an excuse to acquire a valuable collection of dictionaries.

JOHN FULFORD

CPSIA information can be obtained
at www.ICGtesting.com
Printed in the USA
LVHW102127111219
640217LV00008B/160/P

9 780983 187219